Prai

In *Mercy's Power*, Maria Gallagher offers a prayer-fueled new perspective on advocacy for life from conception until natural death. A must-read for pro-life advocates, from the mother sharing ultrasound pictures with her older children, to the Rosary-praying witness outside abortion clinics, and the neighbor who runs errands and shares tea with the senior citizen down the block. Learn how everyone's advocacy is essential to the culture of life.

— **Barb Szyszkiewicz**, writer and editor, CatholicMom.com

Mercy's Power draws inspiration from many teachings and traditions of our Catholic faith to explain the sacredness of each human life and how God calls everyone to defend life in some meaningful way. Having worked closely with Maria Gallagher for more than 20 years in the trenches of the pro-life movement, I can and do attest to the passion she has for life, the veracity of the words she employs so effectively to communicate her profound message, and the sacrifices that she makes every day to respond to God's personal call to her to defend life. Whether you are new to the pro-life cause or a seasoned pro-life activist, Maria offers you knowledge on which to build a foundation for action in the 21st century.

— **Michael V. Ciccocioppo, Jr.**, former Executive Director, Pennsylvania Pro-Life Federation

In *Mercy's Power*, Maria Gallagher sets a practical and doable tone for anyone working for a culture of life in this world. Embellished with her own intimate experiences coupled with the wisdom of the Church, she presents God's Mercy in a way that is alluring, personal, real, and powerful. In these pages, the Face of Divine Mercy that is largely inexplicable and mysterious to us, is revealed in everyday lived experiences and movements of the heart. A helpful guide for everyone who recognizes the need for mercy in their pro-life work.

— **Remil Teny**, co-host of the
"Positively Pro-Life!" podcast

Mercy's Power is the consummate guide for defending life from conception to natural death. Through her engaging and relatable experiences, Maria Gallagher masterfully equips us with the tools, guidance, and inspiration we need for the journey. Be it excerpts from papal encyclicals, discussions about the grace that come from prayer and the Sacraments, or links to pregnancy resources and advocacy programs, everything you need for living out the Gospel of Life is right here at your fingertips with this trusty resource. Emphasizing Divine Mercy's power to fortify us, Maria also wonderfully illustrates its transformative power when poured out on others. A must-read from a superb Ambassador for Life!

— **Claire McGarry**, author of *Grace in Tension:*
Discover Peace with Martha and Mary

MERCY'S POWER

*Inspiration to Serve
the Gospel of Life*

Maria V. Gallagher

Available from:
Marian Helpers Center
Stockbridge, MA 01263
Prayerline: 1-800-804-3823
Orderline: 1-800-462-7426

Websites:
ShopMercy.org
TheDivineMercy.org

Library of Congress Control Number: 2023903832
ISBN 978-1-59614-585-6

Imprimi Potest:
Very Rev. Chris Alar, MIC
Provincial Superior
The Blessed Virgin Mary, Mother of Mercy Province
March 20, 2023
Solemnity of St. Joseph

Nihil Obstat:
Robert A. Stackpole, STD
Censor Deputatus
March 20, 2023

MARIAN PRESS
STOCKBRIDGE MA 01263

This book is dedicated to my parents,
Anne and Dan Vitale, who taught me
the secret of merciful love. Your example
has sparked a flame of hope within me
which will never be extinguished.

"Go and learn the meaning of the words 'I desire mercy, not sacrifice.' I did not come to call the righteous but sinners."

— Matthew 9:13

TABLE OF CONTENTS

Introduction

"Great love can change small things
into great ones, and it is only love
which lends value to our actions."

— Saint Maria Faustina Kowalska[1]

This is a critical time in the history of our world and of our faith — a time when advocates for life must be more persuasive and courageous than ever before. As a result, it occurred to me that we need a spiritual guidebook, one that can provide solace and support during these turbulent times.

We require a handbook for how best to renew the culture of life in an environment that can be quite hostile to our message. While *Roe v. Wade* is now history, a range of threats to innocent human life — from the moment of conception to the twilight of life — persist. Indeed, in some instances, the voices raised against protection of life have grown louder and have been accompanied by violent attacks against churches, pregnancy resource centers, and various faith-based institutions. In the face of such virulent opposition, the need for a manual for spiritual guidance is more necessary than ever.

This is what *Mercy's Power* is designed to be — a trusty companion for our journey. For those who seek to transform the culture, the journey represents both a spiritual climb and a sojourn paved with acts of mercy. Think of it as combining the best of the biblical sisters Mary and Martha — we must be attentive to the Lord, while also extending hospitality to our fellow men and women.

I did not grow up thinking I would become what I like to call "an Ambassador for Life." During my childhood, I considered occupations ranging from hairstylist (my grandfather was a barber) to judge (I watched a lot of law-and-order TV shows). As you will learn, I was also captivated by the idea of becoming a journalist.

As I recall, I did not have a clear picture of abortion until I was in seventh grade and our school principal led us down to the state capitol, where we conducted a silent, prayerful protest against the 1973 United States Supreme Court decision known as *Roe v. Wade*. That single court decision led to the deaths of scores of millions of unborn babies and left their mothers grieving for the children they would never hold in their arms. What a wonderful day it was on June 24, 2022 when the U.S. Supreme Court tossed out *Roe* and declared that abortion policy should be decided by individual states!

At a pivotal point in my life, I received a calling to work that champions Pope St. John Paul II's forward-looking encyclical known as *Evangelium Vitae,* or the *Gospel of Life.* It is work that is powered by prayer. I cannot imagine trying to attempt such a vast undertaking without the aid of the Lord, His Blessed Mother, and all the angels and saints. In addition, the more I studied, the more I became convinced of the need for Divine Mercy to minister to our nation and our world.

The concept of Divine Mercy can be critical for establishing and maintaining a culture of life. An outpouring of Jesus' mercy acts like a healing balm for our souls, helping to strengthen us for the task at hand. In a world where so many suffer from the wounds of the culture of death, Divine Mercy can be the antidote for what ails us.

It is likely that all of us, to a greater or lesser extent, have struggled to overcome the damage caused by an anti-life culture. Some are mothers and fathers who have sacrificed their own children … Some are grandparents who have lost their descendants to abortion. Others have had their families shattered by the horror of assisted suicide … or have had loved ones threatened by euthanasia. Please rest assured of my prayers as you continue on the path to healing and hope.

All of us can serve as wounded healers, using the lessons we have learned about the devastation of death culture to reach out to others who are struggling. Whether you are new to the Christian faith or an old-timer, in these pages you will learn how to channel your faith into peaceful pro-life action. Here, you will find encouragement for your advocacy efforts, whether that takes you to the halls of pregnancy resource centers or to the corridors of your state Capitol.

Our faith compels us to work toward a civilization of love, where every life is cherished and protected. It is a sacred calling that springs forth from our Baptism, by which we became adopted daughters and sons of an all-loving God. Our duty to evangelize means that we must defend human life at all stages — from the moment of conception to the instant of natural death.

To fortify us for the journey, we will begin with a real-life tale of transformation and redemption, which gives us hope that the most vocal opponents of the crusade for life can become ambassadors for the cause of life.

Questions to Ponder

1. To what extent have you done small things with great love this week?

2. How did you come to hold your pro-life beliefs?

3. How have you been wounded by an anti-life culture?

4. In what ways are you a wounded healer?

CHAPTER 1

Conversion of Heart

"Two loves: one good, the other bad; one sweet, the other bitter. The two cannot agree or dwell together in a sinner's heart. It is this, therefore: if anyone loves anything but Thee, O Lord, Thy love is not in him."

— Saint Augustine of Hippo[2]

I came into the world as a result of an unplanned pregnancy. Loved, yes — wholeheartedly, devotedly, by both my mother and my father, but unexpected nonetheless. My mother, who worked as a medical secretary, was fired from her job after her employer found out she was pregnant. But she was determined to bring her unintended blessing into the world.

Labor came fast for my mother — so fast, in fact, that she was unable to make it to the hospital before I made my debut. My father, who had no medical training, delivered me, based on the instructions he received by telephone from the OB/GYN. I suppose his experience in the military also prepared him to act coolly and confidently during an emergency.

Less than two years later, my mother gave birth again, prematurely, to another girl. My sister Terri spent her first few days of life in an incubator, and doctors did not know whether she would survive. But my parents had faith — not only in the medical team, but in the God they had worshipped all their lives. She survived — and thrived — and I was thrilled to have a little sister to call my own.

My father was from a large family, the sixth of seven children. His parents had both immigrated to the United States from Italy and they had held onto their Catholic faith for dear life. His mother was especially vigilant in ensuring that their children be baptized and attend Sunday Mass.

My mother's family had come to the U.S. much earlier, from Ireland. Faith was fundamental in their family, and my mother's maternal aunt was a Sister of St. Joseph. Sister Celestia, whom we knew as Aunt May, was a gentle soul who preached with actions rather than words. Her love for my sister and me was bountiful and beautiful and brightened my days as a child and young adult.

One of the lasting memories of my youth is of my mother holding tight to her Rosary beads. She was insistent that I receive a Catholic education, and both she and my father sacrificed greatly to send me to parochial schools.

This was post-Vatican II and, unfortunately, religious education was largely limited to promoting the ideals of caring and sharing. While these are noble traits to instill in children, they do not tell the full story of the Catholic faith. As a result, I graduated from my Catholic high school having little knowledge or understanding of Catholic moral teaching. In fact, I did not even know that premarital sex was a mortal sin. I did not even know what constituted mortal, or grave sin — transgressions that separate us from the love of God. I knew how to care and share — but not how to share my faith, because I barely knew the fundamental concepts of Catholicism.

But I was an expert in media. From a young age, I watched Congressional hearings on television, listened to radio news reports, and read the newspaper. I regularly watched a sitcom featuring a television news producer and, at the tender age of 10, decided that journalism would be a fitting career path.

I recruited my sister to climb under the dining room table with me, where we pretended to deliver television news reports. I viewed the life of a journalist as exciting and glamorous, and I loved imagining myself appearing on television.

One of our local television stations aired a program devoted to school news, and I made it my mission to make an appearance. I was thrilled to stand in the television studio and make my news debut. I imagined people at home applauding my appearance, and I took great pride in my time in the spotlight.

I envisioned one day becoming a TV correspondent and reporting on the great stories of the day. I could see myself reporting from the United States Capitol, from Moscow, from the war front. I vowed that, wherever the action was, that is where I would be.

I came to journalism quite naturally. My mother had been a high school correspondent for her local city newspaper, and my father had wanted to study journalism in college (The military, however, decided that his aptitude lay in math, so he ended up majoring in accounting.). I rarely, however, thought about my parents' journalistic dreams. I was too busy thinking about my own.

My parents instilled in me a desire to look out for the little guy (or girl). I vividly recall taking on a bully who was picking on one of my classmates. I was willing to stand up for those whom I felt were vulnerable. Eventually, this trait would lead me to speak out on behalf of the voiceless children in the womb and other at-risk populations. But my time as a spokeswoman for preborn children, the elderly, the infirm, and people with disabilities was still a long way off.

I loved to talk as a child and, very early in my school career, I showed a propensity for prose. I wrote so much, in fact, that my fifth-grade Language Arts teacher, Miss Burnett, predicted that I would someday write a book. I wasn't so sure a book was in my future, but I did feel a calling to write.

It never occurred to me to contemplate what course God might want me to take for my life. As was common in those times, the emphasis was on me and my personal vision. I prayed to do well in school and that my father's employer would be able to make payroll so our family wouldn't starve. But I did not pray for guidance. I did not think to ask God what dreams He had for me. I figured He would go along with mine.

When seventh grade came, I had to attend a public middle school, and there I encountered a fierce round of bullying. The school was notorious for tensions and violence, and I was vulnerable. One girl threatened me regularly with a stick pin, and I wondered when the day would come when she would prick me and I would bleed. Other girls made fun of the scapular I wore around my neck — a modest sacramental in honor of Our Lady. Because I was showing my allegiance to Mary, the girls claimed that I was a "devil worshipper."

One day in gym class, when we were doing tumbling, I managed to injure my neck. My neck became so stiff I could not move my head from side to side. Apparently, I had sprained it in my futile attempt at gymnastics. I told my mother I simply could not return to the middle school. I had finally reached my breaking point.

My mother was beside herself with worry, wondering what to do with me. An educator suggested she consider homeschooling, but my mother was uncomfortable teaching and knew it would not work out. She could not afford to send me back to the first Catholic school I attended, and she had to rule out the second one because of the bullying.

Frustrated, my mother turned to the phone book and looked through the listings for schools. She happened to find a lay-run Catholic school with traditional teaching. While the principal was wary of accepting a new girl into the seventh grade, she agreed to let me have a "test run."

I came to fall in love with Mater Dei Academy and with the Catholic faith. I felt safe, knowing that the students followed established rules and that bullying was not tolerated. The curriculum was challenging, and the teachers required the best of each of us. I had never experienced such a welcoming learning environment before, and I was greatly blessed by it.

Sister Eunice gave us a religion quiz every week, and promised a hamburger to anyone who scored 100 percent. With that incentive, I aced the tests and looked forward to my weekly treat. Unfortunately, I quickly forgot the material after the test. This might explain why, as a young adult, I was perplexed by the notions of mortal, or grave sins, and venial, or lesser sins. Also, I was only at Mater Dei for a year and a half, which is not much time to learn the fullness of the Catholic faith.

Our principal, Mrs. Clark, was also our primary teacher. The mother of a large brood, she was kind but firm, determined to impart to us a sound education. I recall one time in particular when Mrs. Clark was teaching us about morality. She drew a line on the blackboard that connected the words "abortion" and "euthanasia." She was trying to show how disrespect for the dawn of life led to disrespect at the twilight of life. I never forgot that legalizing abortion put our nation on a slippery slope which led to euthanasia. At the time, however, I wondered, "How on earth could anyone ever kill Grandma?" The idea that an elderly person's life would be snuffed out in a misguided act of mercy seemed revolting to me.

Mrs. Clark issued an invitation to me, one that would have a profound influence on my life. She invited me to join the pro-life movement in 1978 when I was just shy of 13 years of age. She boldly led our class to the state Capitol, where we staged our own demonstration one bitterly cold January day. We were protesting the legalization of abortion under the tragic U.S. Supreme Court ruling known as *Roe v. Wade*.

As I stood shivering with my sign, I wondered, "Where are all the people?" I had no knowledge of the annual March for Life, which attracted hundreds of thousands of individuals each year to Washington, D.C. on the anniversary of *Roe*. My parents were not involved in the pro-life movement, and I have no recollection of them discussing abortion when my sister and I were children. I believe now that my mother wanted to shield me from that harsh, unjust reality.

Looking back, I believe that that student protest was my initial call to the pro-life movement. I knew it was a profound event, and it had a deep effect on me. I recognized that my life had been changed by it.

But what was next? Where would I take my pro-life activism? Unfortunately, as I got older, I lost my passion for the pro-life cause, in a detour that took me onto a rocky new path — but one that many young women my age would also travel.

I still remember the trepidation I experienced writing my first article for my high school newspaper, *The Hawkeye*. I was assigned to write about a spaghetti dinner fundraiser for our Catholic high school, Bishop Hartley. Because I was a perfectionist, I labored over every word. Because I lacked confidence, I enlisted one of my best friends, Theresa, to co-write the piece.

Still, I liked the idea of being a student journalist. I graduated to writing feature articles about trendy topics ranging from professional wrestling to television watching. It never seemed to occur to me that my faith should inform my writing — that I, in fact, could become an even better writer if I allowed the Holy Spirit to be my guide. I had a decidedly secular approach to this extra-curricular activity, which would ultimately lead me away from the teachings of the Catholic faith.

I still harbored dreams of appearing on the Broadway stage, and yet, I did not like the life of insecurity that awaited a struggling actor. It seemed to me that my ticket to job security rested in majoring in journalism in college. So, with that goal in mind, I enrolled at nearby Ohio State University when I graduated from high school.

I loved learning about the early days of journalism in the colonies — the publications that helped to form the foundation of the United States. I believed strongly that journalism was a noble profession and that I could change the world for the better by pursuing it. I was idealistic and on a mission, and I looked forward to the opportunity of working as a reporter.

As a prerequisite to my television journalism classes, I had to take courses in radio reporting and production. At the time, I didn't understand why — I had no interest in a radio career and was anxious to begin life as a television journalist.

I distinctly recall sitting in the radio news lab, at the desk of my instructor. A Catholic who no longer attended church, he told me that he was "prochoice" on the issue of abortion. Even though I have no artistic ability whatsoever, I drew him a picture of a baby in a mother's womb, asking him how he could argue against that. In that moment, I engaged in what I would later learn was pro-life apologetics.

Shortly thereafter, a position opened up at the campus radio station. The station was looking for an undergraduate who could serve as student reporter on the weekends. Even though I still did not harbor any aspirations for radio work, I decided to apply. I felt a little funny about it — the hours were 8 a.m. to 6 p.m., both Saturday and Sunday. I wasn't sure how I would fit Sunday Mass into the equation.

But my parents were still struggling financially, and I thought this was an opportunity to help out. I also envisioned that the experience would enable me to land a television job after graduation. So, I accepted the position — not realizing that radio journalism would change me in ways that would make it even harder to find God.

In the beginning, I tried to make sure that I "fit in" Sunday Mass at 7 a.m., before my shift at the radio station began. But I was also committed to my social calendar, and campus parties often lasted into the wee hours of the morning. As a result, there were times when I overslept and never made it to Mass.

I knew that my absences at Mass bothered my mother greatly. She had worked so hard to instill the faith in me, and she saw it slipping away. I was so focused on my work and my studies that I failed to see that I was stepping away from God. I thought I needed to be busy about the business of earning a living — and learning the skills necessary to land a better job in the future. It did not occur to me to consider what impact my workaholic ways were having on my spiritual life.

At the radio station, I learned that the Associated Press stylebook was the bible of the journalism industry. The stylebook offered preferred ways of wording various issues. The term "pro-life" was banned. We were, instead, supposed to use a phrase such as "opponents of abortion rights." The phrase "pro-abortion" was also prohibited. We were required to refer to those supporting legal abortion as proponents of "abortion rights."

The language requirements of my employer affected the way that I thought about the entire issue of abortion. I was now focused on "women's rights" rather than the rights of the preborn child. Since my prayer life also suffered greatly during this time period, I was not seeking the enlightenment of God when writing my stories. While I held fast to some teachings of the Church — such as those on poverty, street violence, and unjust wars — I ignored others.

Rather than evangelizing — what all Catholics are called to do — the secular journalism culture was evangelizing me. Slowly, seemingly imperceptibly, I was abandoning my pro-life convictions. I reasoned that some religions approved of abortion and even thought that the Catholic Church might someday think the same. If asked, I would have labelled myself as "pro-choice," not realizing that many women report feeling pressured to abort, thinking that they have no other choice. In reality, many people who call themselves "pro-choice" are actually not in favor of abortion for any reason during all nine months of pregnancy.

Sadly, I had abandoned that girl who bravely stood in protest of abortion. I was now a "modern girl" immersed in modern journalism. I had slipped into a different world — and I ultimately would find it hard to get out.

I can only speculate that it was my mother's prayers that led me to begin reading pro-life works — largely out of curiosity. A friend had asked what I was doing for the pro-life cause. I had replied that there was nothing I could do, since I was a journalist. He began supplying me with pro-life materials to peruse. I found myself captivated by the concept of fetal development — something that had been unknown to me at this point, even though I had covered many a story dealing with abortion.

The more I read, the more I became convinced that life did, indeed, begin at conception. I could not escape this scientific fact — even after all the pro-abortion rhetoric in which I had been immersed.

My heart began to break for the lives lost to abortion — and for the role my biased reporting may have played in that. I decided to participate in a pro-life Rosary procession sponsored by my parish; with each "Hail Mary" that I uttered, I became more convinced of the rightness of the pro-life cause.

At an Irish dancing festival in the Catskills, of all places, I heard an unforgettable homily from an Irish priest, passionately and convincingly speaking about the outrageousness of abortion. I wept and, in the midst of that flood of tears, I vowed that I needed to do more to safeguard human life. I would end up dedicating my life to the cause of defending the most vulnerable, toiling full-time in the vineyards of the pro-life movement. I gave up my journalism career to work full-time in the areas of pro-life education and advocacy. It was a decision I would never regret.

Questions to Ponder

1. Have you ever experienced a conversion of heart? What prompted your transformation?

2. Do you believe that God is calling you to a conversion of heart now? Why or why not?

3. Have you ever made your work into an idol? If so, how might you remedy the situation?

4. Do you feel a calling to become involved, or more involved, in the pro-life movement? What would be the obstacles in your life right now that might need to be overcome if you felt God was calling you to become more involved in the pro-life movement?

Chapter 2

The Quest for Holiness

"Strive for peace with everyone,
and for that holiness without
which no one will see the Lord."

— Hebrews 12:14

I carry with me a picture within my mind — a portrait from long ago. In it, as a toddler, I am clinging to my mother in the church of my Baptism. It is Christmastime, and the little church is decorated with festive flair. I do not know all that is going on — the Mass remains a profound mystery to me. And yet, I am filled with a feeling of unadulterated joy.

In that moment of decades past, I am in touch with the living God. It is as if He has wrapped His arms around me and refuses to let go. I feel safe, loved, and cared for. It is as if I am the only human being on planet Earth and He, my heavenly Father, is cradling me — His beloved daughter.

I would grow up to be the prodigal daughter, fascinated with the world and allowing my relationship to God to wither. While He was steadfast, I would wriggle out of His embrace, running after the promises of the world while ignoring the pledges my Lord had made to me. It was a lonely existence, trying to negotiate the twists and turns of life without the Father's guidance.

I pursued my journalism career with a laser-like intensity, making it into the idol of my affection. I was working as many as 15 hours a day, barely making time for sleep and meals. The happiness that I thought my news reporting jobs would bring me was fleeting. Sometimes, I would lie awake at night, thinking I was destined to spend eternal life in hell. It would be years before I recognized the healing balm that a good confession could provide to my wounded soul.

After making a retreat at my parents' parish and returning to the Sacrament of Reconciliation, I began praying more often. This practice gradually led me to daily recitation of the Most Holy Rosary — an opportunity to meditate on the life of Christ and His mother Mary (For more on how to make the Rosary come alive in your life, please consult my previous book, *Joyful Encounters with Mary* [Marian Press, 2022]).

The *Catechism of the Catholic Church* makes it clear that all of us are called to become saints: "'All Christians in any state or walk of life are called to the fullness of Christian life and to the perfection of charity.' All are called to holiness: 'Be perfect, as your heavenly Father is perfect.'"[3]

Holiness can be achieved only through God's grace and mercy. But we must do our part by cultivating a consistent and faithful prayer life. With the busyness of modern life, this can be quite challenging. But it is indeed possible if we make a commitment to reach out to the Lord in prayer.

As we look to renew a culture of life, we can view the undertaking as if we are working to build an exquisite cathedral. In order to make the project become a reality, we need a blueprint. God provides the blueprint, and we access it through prayer. As we read in Psalm 127, "Unless the Lord build the house, they labor in vain who build."

If we read on to verses 3 and 4 of Psalm 127, we learn of the value God places on children: "Certainly sons are a gift from the Lord, the fruit of the womb, a reward. Like arrows in the hand of a warrior are the sons born in one's youth." In this way, Scripture emphasizes the sanctity of human life and the incredible blessing of children in our lives.

While prayer may be essential to our efforts advocating for human life, the question remains: How do we become adept at prayer? I recall during a particularly challenging time in my life, I phoned an acquaintance from a support group to ask, "How do you pray?" I had become so obsessed with the difficult circumstances that I was facing that I had forgotten how to communicate with God.

Today I turn to the *Catechism* for guidance on how best to get in touch with the Lord. I mine the spiritual treasures within its pages in order to discover ways to strengthen my relationship with the Almighty.

BLESSING

The *Catechism* notes that "Blessing" is the foundation of prayer — the encounter between the Lord and human beings. "The prayer of blessing is man's response to God's gifts: because God blesses, the human heart can in return bless the One who is the source of every blessing."[4]

Blessing is essentially a two-way street: Our prayer rises to the Father through Christ in the Holy Spirit — "we bless Him for having blessed us." Meanwhile, God blesses us as grace rains down on us from the Father through Christ by means of the Holy Spirit.[5]

I know that I could spend an eternity contemplating the blessings that God has bestowed upon me: loving parents, a vivacious and talented daughter, and a devoted sister, not to mention fulfilling work, caring friends, a vibrant church community — the list is endless. It is an attitude of gratitude that can draw us closer to God and help our love to grow for our neighbor.

ADORATION

I can recall an incident when I was very young, on a summer drive with my mother. As I stared at the parade of trees passing by my car window, I was overwhelmed by the majesty of God. It was a truly awe-inspiring moment — a moment when I wordlessly adored the God Who is the Author of Life.

As the *Catechism* teaches, adoration "is the first attitude of man acknowledging that he is a creature before his Creator. It exalts the greatness of the Lord who made us and the almighty power of the Savior who sets us free from evil."[6]

To adore is to give homage — the respect that is due our heavenly King. We recognize our littleness before His greatness. Adoration requires a certain degree of humility, an understanding that we stand in the shadow of our Maker.

PETITION

From an early age, I had a list of requests for the Almighty that, if printed out on sheets of paper, could have wallpapered the bedroom I shared with my sister. I yearned for many things and experiences — a house rather than our cramped two-bedroom apartment … heightened skills at playing kickball … a trio of friends I could call besties. I saw God as my ultimate Provider and the One to turn to in order to satisfy my yearnings.

The *Catechism* speaks to this desire of our hearts:

> The vocabulary of supplication in the New Testament is rich in shades of meaning: ask, beseech, plead, invoke, entreat, cry out, even "struggle in prayer." Its most usual form, because the most spontaneous, is petition: by prayer of petition we express awareness of our relationship with God. We are creatures who are not our own beginning, not the masters of adversity, not our own last end. We are sinners who as Christians know that we have turned away from our Father. Our petition is already a turning back to Him.[7]

When I was a child, presenting to the Lord my litany of petitions, I was missing a key element — a request for forgiveness. As the *Catechism* states:

> The first movement of the prayer of petition is *asking forgiveness,* like the tax collector in the parable: "God, be merciful to me a sinner!" It is a prerequisite for righteous and pure prayer. A trusting humility brings us back into the light of communion between the Father and his Son Jesus Christ and with one another, so that "we receive from him whatever we ask." Asking forgiveness is the prerequisite for both the Eucharistic liturgy and personal prayer.[8]

The true beauty of prayer is that it establishes a relationship of trust with God, so that we can cast all of our cares upon Him, knowing that He will do what is best for us. The *Catechism* emphasizes the steadfastness of God's abiding love:

> When we share in God's saving love, we understand that *every need* can become the object of petition. Christ, who assumed all things in order to redeem all things, is glorified by what we ask the Father in his name. It is with this confidence that St. James and St. Paul exhort us to pray *at all times.*[9]

The exhortation of St. James and St. Paul can be a stumbling block for many of us. With all of our responsibilities — from earning a living to raising children and assisting grandchildren — we may feel as if we lack the time to pray as we should. That is why I find *The Morning Offering* so helpful. With this request to the Father, I offer all of my prayers, actions, and sacrifices back to Him each day in an offering of love. We can also pray a decade of the Rosary while we are waiting in a drive-thru line or biding time in a queue at the bank. Indeed, the various "waiting periods" we encounter during the day may be invitations to prayer.

INTERCESSION

In recent years, one of my favorite types of prayer has been intercession. Using this form of prayer, we model Jesus, who acts as an Intercessor with the Father on behalf of others. As the *Catechism* points out, intercession actually predates the Incarnation, when Jesus came to earth to save us from our sins:

> Since Abraham, intercession — asking on behalf of another — has been characteristic of a heart attuned to God's mercy. In the age of the Church, Christian intercession participates in Christ's, as an expression of the communion of saints. In intercession, he who prays looks "not only to his own interests, but also to the interests of others," even to the point of praying for those who do him harm.[10]

The *Catechism* goes on to say that "the intercession of Christians recognizes no boundaries."[11] In other words, we pray not only on behalf of people who are good to us, but on behalf of those who persecute us.

I have found this practice to be quite comforting, especially as it relates to the cause of life. We pray for pregnant mothers in their time of need, as well as for the fathers of those preborn babies. But we are also called to pray for those who stand in opposition to our cause, including those who work in abortion facilities and public officials who promote and vote to fund abortion with our tax dollars.

In fact, praying for our persecutors can help to humanize them in our eyes, enabling us to realize that they are our brothers and sisters and that they are also worthy of love and respect.

THANKSGIVING

At one time I associated Thanksgiving with a single day each year, begun with a perfunctory prayer and topped off with a not-so-healthy portion of turkey and stuffing. It was the only time I prayed before a meal — or gave much thought to giving thanks to God for my many blessings.

As I progressed along the ladder of life, my perspective shifted. I began to realize that I needed to thank the good Lord every day — not only for my meals, but for the many other instances of good fortune that came my way.

According to the *Catechism*:

As in the prayer of petition, every event and need can become an offering of thanksgiving. The letters of St. Paul often begin and end with thanksgiving, and the Lord Jesus is always present in it: "Give thanks in all circumstances; for this is the will of God in Christ Jesus for you"; "Continue steadfastly in prayer, being watchful in it with thanksgiving."[12]

Since I have been deliberate about prayers of thanksgiving, I have developed a greater trust in God because I can recognize the many blessings He has bestowed upon me. I no longer believe I am wanting for anything, since I know without a doubt that He is looking out for me.

PRAISE

I once heard a story about a judicial nominee who, in the midst of a media firestorm, would go home, turn off the news, and listen to nothing but praise-and-worship music. He found solace in the sweet melodies and stirring lyrics, and the uplifting tunes helped him to pray and gave him the strength to power through a contentious confirmation fight.

I also find that, when I am at my lowest point, emotionally-speaking, music can be just the medicine I need to combat what ails me. It is just so soothing to listen to spiritual music and to let the waves of sound carry me away from my troubles.

In fact, when I share my difficulties with a particular friend, she invariably responds, "Keep praising God." While it may seem counter-intuitive, praising God in the midst of a mess is actually quite freeing. It helps me to take my eyes off circumstances for a while and re-focus on the Lord, who is the ultimate source of my joy.

The *Catechism* explains praise this way:

Praise is the form of prayer which recognizes most immediately that God is God. It lauds God for His own sake and gives him glory, quite beyond what he does, but simply because HE IS. It shares in the blessed happiness of the pure of heart who love God in faith before seeing him in glory.[13]

Through praise, I can reach out and glorify God, even as I struggle with various trials and tribulations. Just knowing that God is near is a source of profound consolation. I feel a greater sense of confidence, knowing that the Lord is at my side and is helping me to carry my cross.

As we grow in our prayer life, we form a firm foundation for our efforts at pro-life advocacy. The closer we are to Christ, the better ambassadors for life we will be. By our fruits the world will know us and will recognize the rightness of our cause.

Questions to Ponder:

1. To what extent is prayer a priority in your life right now?

2. How could you go about finding more time for prayer in your day?

3. What is your favorite form of prayer and why?

4. Which type of prayer might you consider adding to your routine this week?

Chapter 3

Food for the Journey

"Jesus said to them, 'I am the bread of life; whoever comes to me will never hunger, and whoever believes in me will never thirst.' "

— John 6:35

My mother treated my First Holy Communion as if it were a wedding. She made sure that our celebration was epic — a sumptuous post-liturgy feast at a local Italian restaurant. My Grandma Hazel was on hand to ensure that the party favors were neatly arranged at every seat. It was the most important event of my young life, and my family honored it accordingly.

According to the *Catechism*, the Eucharist is "the source and summit of the Christian life."[14]

That is an intriguing phrase — one that merits our attention. Out of our reception of Holy Communion, our Christian life flows. The Holy Eucharist represents the pinnacle of our lives here on earth — the greatest gift we can receive. Indeed, our work as ambassadors for life can grow and prosper through the Eucharist.

As the *Catechism* states:

> The other sacraments, and indeed all ecclesiastical ministries and works of the apostolate, are bound up with the Eucharist and are oriented toward it. For in the blessed Eucharist is contained the whole spiritual good of the Church, namely Christ himself, our Pasch.[15]

The Eucharist is the Body and Blood of Christ and, through this Sacrament, we are united with Jesus in a profound way: "the Eucharist is the sum and summary of our faith: 'Our way of thinking is attuned to the Eucharist, and the Eucharist in turn confirms our way of thinking.'"[16]

The Eucharist is heavenly food for our spiritual journey. Holy Communion gives us the sustenance we need to fortify ourselves for the many challenges presented by efforts to renew our culture.

It is noteworthy to point out that the late Fr. John Hardon, SJ stated, "There is no stopping abortion without the Eucharist. . . . Everything depends on our faith — in the measure that we believe that the living God who made heaven and earth is on earth and [has] the same humanity which He received from His Virgin Mother. In that measure we shall convert the culture of death to the culture of life." [17]

When I was the co-coordinator of a parish pro-life group, one of the first activities we established was a weekly Holy Hour for the success of our apostolic efforts. During our hour of adoration before the Blessed Sacrament, we joined together in prayer and song, beseeching the Lord for His guidance as we reached out to pregnant mothers facing challenging circumstances. I felt a tremendous sense of peace during those Holy Hours, experiencing the reality of God's presence as we prepared to embark on our holy work. While the pro-life movement is the civil rights movement of our time, it is also a movement sustained and motivated by prayer. And those prayers have particular urgency when invoked before the Blessed Sacrament.

The *Catechism*, in quoting Pope St. John Paul II, attests to the power and efficacy of adoration before the Sacred Host:

> The Church and the world have a great need for Eucharistic worship. Jesus awaits us in this sacrament of love. Let us not refuse the time to go to meet him in adoration, in contemplation full of faith, and open to making amends for the serious offenses and crimes of the world. Let our adoration never cease.[18]

How many times do we overlook or dismiss this "sacrament of love"? I remember a time when I was a young adult and was surprised by the crowd that had gathered one Friday night for an evening of adoration. I wondered why people would give up a night on the town to pray before the Sacred Host. While I knew about the Real Presence, my appreciation for the Eucharist had waned since my First Holy Communion years before.

And yet, on that pivotal night, grace touched my heart. I realized that I had experienced something profound in gazing upon the Sacred Host and it was an experience I longed to repeat. In this way, God rekindled my love for the Eucharist — a spark which remains with me to this day.

Not long after that (and not surprisingly) I became a daily Communicant. I desired to receive my Lord as often as I could — and waiting from one Sunday to the next seemed unbearable. When I am not able to get to church physically, I watch a livestream of the Mass on my computer and opt for a Spiritual Communion, asking Jesus into my heart and soul.

My home diocese, the Harrisburg diocese in Pennsylvania, offers the following explanation from Fr. Hardon of the benefits of a Spiritual Communion:

> For those who are unable to receive the Body and Blood of Jesus in Holy Communion, making a conscious desire that Jesus come spiritually into your soul is called a spiritual communion. Spiritual Communion can be made through an act of faith and love throughout one's day and it is highly commended to us by the Church.

According to the Catechism of the Council of Trent, the faithful who "receive the Eucharist in spirit" are "those who, inflamed with a lively faith that works in charity, partake in wish and desire of the celestial Bread offered to them, receive from it, if not the entire, at least very great benefits." (cf. Fr. John Hardon, SJ, *Modern Catholic Dictionary*)[19]

A day does not go by without me either receiving the Body and Blood of Christ or making a Spiritual Communion. I have made union with our Lord and Savior a top priority of my day, and I am always grateful for the opportunity to receive Him into my soul. The practice has transformed my life and can dramatically change your life as well.

Questions to Ponder

1. If you have received the Sacrament of Holy Communion, what do you recall about your first experience receiving the Body and Blood of Christ?

2. What experience have you had with adoration of the Blessed Sacrament?

3. What would it take for you to add Spiritual Communions to your day?

4. In what ways do you view Holy Communion as "the sacrament of love?"

Chapter 4

Healing the Heart

"If a piece of canvas painted upon
by an artist could think and speak, it
certainly would not complain at being
constantly touched and retouched by
the brush, and would not envy the lot
of that instrument, for it would realize
it was not to the brush but to the artist
using it that it owed the beauty with
which it was clothed."

— Saint Thérèse of Lisieux[20]

Each of us is a masterpiece, created lovingly by the Father's Hand. And yet, through the effects of sin — both our own transgressions and those of other people — our hearts can be damaged. While we may always carry scars, the breakage can be healed through God's loving touch.

Perhaps even more amazingly, we can become wounded healers — reaching out to others with compassion and care. I am reminded of women who have suffered the tragedy of abortion and, in the aftermath of their sorrow, extend a helping hand to pregnant women in crisis. Their grief at the loss of their children is profound, and they work diligently to help prevent other women from suffering the same tragic ordeal.

Such is the case with a woman I know named Becky. She founded a ministry called Undefeated Courage, based on her desire to help other women avoid the abortion trap:

> Unfortunately I learned the hard way. With two abortions by age 16 and over twenty-five years of grief, guilt and regret, I no longer wanted to live with the thought that I willingly aborted two of my children. I didn't know better back then. I was forced to choose abortion. I went through with it because I didn't feel that I had any other choice.
>
> Until one day at my afternoon job at a local hospital where I was asked to sort through fetal remains from a local abortion center to confirm a successful abortion procedure. I sat there counting parts of babies, holding their tiny hands and feet between my thumb and index finger. In that moment, my eyes were opened to what I had done. I cried over those babies. I sobbed for my own. But I continued to hide from that reality for over two decades

more, carrying my heavy burden alone. I pretended everything was fine. But it, and I, was not.

Until one day, I went with my church group to visit the local abortion center to pray for the clients inside — and found myself on my knees, crying, begging for forgiveness — and help. I found both through those friends that day — and healing later through a Rachel's Vineyard retreat.[21] And in March of 2014, Undefeated Courage was born out of my desire to help others who need someone to offer hope and a way out, too.[22]

Through Undefeated Courage, Becky offers practical assistance to pregnant women — including free ultrasounds through a mobile ultrasound unit. The nonjudgmental support is just what many women need to summon up the courage and strength to choose life for their unborn babies.

Jesus, the Divine Healer, stands ready to bind up our wounds. He offered words of comfort to St. Maria Faustina Kowalska, as she recorded in her diary, *Divine Mercy in My Soul:*

All grace flows from mercy ... even if a person's sins were as dark as night, God's mercy is stronger than our misery. One thing alone is necessary: that the sinner

set ajar the door of his heart, be it ever
so little, to let in a ray of God's merciful
grace, and then God will do the rest.[23]

All too often, we may feel as if our sins are
unforgiveable, that our failings are outside of the
realm of God's mercy. But that is not the reality of
the situation. As Jesus told Faustina:

> **I am love and mercy itself. ... Let no soul
> fear to draw near to Me, even though
> its sins be as scarlet. ... My mercy is
> greater than your sins, and those of the
> entire world. ... I let My Sacred Heart
> be pierced with a lance, thus opening
> wide the source of mercy for you. Come
> then with trust to draw graces from this
> fountain ... The graces of My mercy are
> drawn by the means of one vessel only,
> and that is — trust. The more a soul
> trusts, the more it will receive. [24]**

If we are honest with Jesus, if we are willing to
speak to Him about our emotional wounds, He can
point us toward the path of healing. In my own life, I
have struggled with a fiery temperament that I once
attributed solely to my genes. After much prayer and
reflection, I recognized that anxiety and unresolved
anger were prompting me to verbally lash out at
family members, friends, and acquaintances. When I
came to realize the source of my sinfulness, I began

to change my response to situations that would have previously earned my ire.

The angry outbursts subsided, and I was more serene as a result. I credit this healing to an outpouring of Divine Mercy in my life.

In the struggle to renew our culture, we must first undergo a personal renewal. If we are not drawing closer to Christ, chances are we are pulling farther away. Our own conversion of heart is absolutely critical if we are to effect positive change in our communities. We must submit ourselves to the Master Artist, allowing His grace to perform the ultimate spiritual makeover.

 Questions to Ponder

1. What experiences have you had with women who have sought abortions?

2. To what extent have you contributed to the culture of death, either intentionally or unintentionally?

3. Do you have emotional wounds that require the healing of the Divine Physician?

4. What are some ways that you can seek emotional healing this week?

Chapter 5

A Mother's Touch

**"Mary is Mother of Mercy because
her Son, Jesus Christ, was sent by the
Father as the revelation of God's mercy
(cf Jn 3:16-18)."**

— Pope St. John Paul II[25]

I have long been an enthusiastic member of Team Mary. The Blessed Mother is my patron saint and I learned as a child to invoke her intercession. I do not believe it was a coincidence that, once I began praying a daily Rosary as an adult, I launched my advocacy for unborn babies and their mothers. Mary led me to Jesus, and Jesus led me to the pro-life movement.

Mary is also a patroness of the pro-life movement, often under the title of Our Lady of Guadalupe. The Blessed Mother appeared on Tepeyac Hill in the year 1531 to a Mexican peasant named Juan Diego. The farmer experienced several visions of Our Lady. During one such appearance, she affirmed her role as Mother of Mercy:

> "I am your merciful mother, the merciful mother of all of you who live united in

this land, and of all mankind, of all those who love me, of those who cry to me, of those who seek me, of those who have confidence in me. Here I will hear their weeping, their sorrow, and will remedy and alleviate all their multiple sufferings, necessities and misfortunes."[26]

It makes sense that we should have recourse to the Blessed Mother as we go about the work of healing our culture from the devastation caused by an anti-life mentality. As a girl facing an unexpected pregnancy, Mary modeled the trusting acceptance and grace that we should all try to imitate.

The *Catechism* explains the special role of Mary in salvation history:

From among the descendants of Eve, God chose the Virgin Mary to be the mother of his Son. "Full of grace," Mary is "the most excellent fruit of redemption" (SC 103): from the first instant of her conception, she was totally preserved from the stain of original sin and she remained pure from all personal sin throughout her life.[27]

Meanwhile, while standing at the foot of Christ's Cross, Mary demonstrated her commitment to her beloved Son — a commitment which would lead to her serving as a mother to all mankind. As we read in John 19:26-27:

When Jesus saw His mother and the disciple there whom he loved, he said to his mother, "Woman, behold, your son." Then he said to the disciple, "Behold, your mother." And from that hour the disciple took her into his home.

But Mary's devotion to mankind did not end with her earthly life. As the *Catechism* points out, the Blessed Mother continues in Heaven her work on our behalf:

This motherhood of Mary in the order of grace continues uninterruptedly from the consent which she loyally gave at the Annunciation and which she sustained without wavering beneath the cross, until the eternal fulfillment of all the elect. Taken up to heaven she did not lay aside this saving office but by her manifold intercession continues to bring us the gifts of eternal salvation … Therefore the Blessed Virgin is invoked in the Church under the titles of Advocate, Helper, Benefactress, and Mediatrix.[28]

It is therefore fitting that we should ask for Mary's protection for all children in the womb, for their precious mothers, and for their often forgotten fathers. When we seek to place individuals in the Blessed Mother's loving arms, we are extending to them the care of the world's perfect mother. Under her guidance, miracles can occur.

As the *Catechism* states, Mary is the Mother of the Church; consequently, it is appropriate for us to seek her intercession for all our needs:

> Since the Virgin Mary's role in the mystery of Christ and the Spirit has been treated, it is fitting now to consider her place in the mystery of the Church. "The Virgin Mary ... is acknowledged and honored as being truly the Mother of God and of the redeemer ... She is 'clearly the mother of the members of Christ' ... since she has by her charity joined in bringing about the birth of believers in the Church, who are members of its head."[29]

If you are a convert to the faith, or if you experienced a strained relationship with your own mother, devotion to Mary may seem like a foreign concept. After all, you might say, can't we just deal directly with God? It is true that God listens to every prayer and answers it in the way He knows to be best. But He has also entrusted us to Mary, who can act as an advocate on our behalf.

You may have been the beneficiary of your own earthly mother's prayers. There is something especially beautiful, especially stirring, about the prayers of a mother for her children. As the ideal mother, Mary can be a particularly effective intercessor for us.

Devotion to the Blessed Mother is essential for transforming our society to one that universally respects human life. The *Catechism* notes the integral role Marian devotion plays in Christianity:

> "The Church's devotion to the Blessed Mother is intrinsic to Christian worship." The Church rightly honors "the Blessed Virgin with special devotion. From the most ancient times the Blessed Virgin has been honored with the title of 'Mother of God,' to whose protection the faithful fly in all their dangers and needs … This very special devotion differs essentially from the adoration which is given to the incarnate Word and equally to the Father and the Holy Spirit, and greatly fosters this adoration."[30]

Mary is always ready to extend a listening ear. As St. Bernardine of Siena said, "You must know that when you 'hail' Mary, she immediately greets you! … If you greet her, she will answer you right away and converse with you!"[31]

But how can we foster a devotion to the Blessed Mother — someone we cannot see? Perhaps the best way is to pray the Holy Rosary, a meditative prayer where we implore the intercession of Mary through the Joyful, Sorrowful, Luminous, and Glorious Mysteries. The Rosary processions outside of abortion facilities throughout the world are a testament to the power of this prayer to change minds and save lives.

A daily Rosary can be a powerful means of cultivating a culture of life in your community. In the U.S. alone, a number of abortion centers have shut their doors following the recitation of many Rosaries for their closures.

Keep in mind the words of St. (Padre) Pio of Pietrelcina, who said, "Our Lady has never refused me a grace through the recitation of the rosary."[32]

In addition, the Rosary can help with our own sanctification, which can enhance our capabilities as ambassadors of life.

As Pope Leo XIII said, "The Rosary is the most excellent form of prayer and the most efficacious means of attaining eternal life. It is the remedy for all our evils, the root of all our blessings. There is no more excellent way of praying."[33]

If you need any more incentive to make the daily Rosary a habit, consider the words of Pope Pius XI:

> If you desire peace in your hearts, in your homes, and in your country, assemble each evening to recite the Rosary. Let not even one day pass without saying it, no matter how burdened you may be with many cares and labors.[34]

Another important way to draw closer to Mary is through consecration to her Immaculate Heart.

The book *33 Days to Morning Glory* by Fr. Michael Gaitley, MIC (Marian Press, 2012), offers step-by-step instructions for making this life-changing consecration. Through the consecration, we give everything over to Mary, to use as she wills. That includes both our temporal and our spiritual goods.

I recall during a particularly difficult time in my life, an older gentleman explained the consecration to me. "You see that coffee cup?" he said, pointing to the drinking vessel on the table. "That belongs to Mary. Everything belongs to her." He further explained that any money he possessed really belonged to the Blessed Mother, so he needed to be a good steward of the funds in his bank account on Mary's behalf. It was a life lesson I have taken to heart and that I try to practice each day.

Why commit to Marian consecration? Aside from the incredible privilege of strengthening our relationship with the Blessed Mother, consecration aids us in our ultimate goal — to arrive at Heaven. This is because Mary wants all of her children to be with her forever, and does not want a single one to be lost. She, working in concert with Christ, will guide us on the path that leads to paradise.

Questions to Ponder:

1. How would you describe your current relationship with the Blessed Mother?

2. What are some wounds from the past that might be hindering your relationship with Mary?

3. Which specific pro-life concerns can you bring to Mary this week?

4. What graces have you received as a result of praying for Mary's intercession?

Chapter 6

Spiritual Mentors

*"The loveliest masterpiece of the heart
of God is the heart of a mother."*

— Saint Thérèse of Lisieux[35]

My first spiritual mentor was my mother. A
life-long Catholic and dedicated prayer
warrior, she ensured that I attended Sunday Mass,
learned my prayers, and received a religious education at parochial schools. It is hard for me to imagine
my spiritual life without her.

Next in importance was my Aunt May, known
in her convent as Sister Celestia. A spiritual mother
to me, Aunt May shared with me the sublime gift of
living a grace-filled life. She was filled with an ethe-
real joy that was contagious, often spread through
peals of laughter. Her spirit of whimsy taught me that
it was indeed possible to be close to God while maintaining a sense of humor about life on planet Earth.

My godmother, Mary, was a constant fixture in
my young life. She came to visit us every Christmas,
a lovely gift for me in tow. She attended each of the
major spiritual milestones of my childhood: First
Holy Communion and Confirmation. While having

no children of her own, she served as a mother figure for me as I was growing up — and growing in the faith.

As I matured, I discovered holy men and women from around the world who had passed from this life — but who could still serve as spiritual mentors to me from their vantage point in the Communion of the Saints. Some have already achieved the sainthood title, while others have not been officially canonized. All bear some connection to the pro-life movement and can aid us as we work to revitalize our society.

SAINT TERESA OF CALCUTTA

I first saw her on a television screen — a diminutive sister in a sari, ministering to the poorest of the poor on the streets of Calcutta, India. To me, she was the holiest person on the planet, willing to care for those who had been abandoned by the rest of the human race. And her smile was ever-present and communicated the love of God in a way that mere words could not.

The woman then known the world over as Mother Teresa became my spiritual mentor from afar. I followed her exploits as she spread her ministry and her message around the globe. I was particularly captivated when she received the Nobel Peace Prize for her selfless work in the slums of her adopted country.

In her speech, Mother Teresa recalled a man she had rescued from the streets:

He was covered with maggots; his face was the only place that was clean. And yet that man, when we brought him to our home for the dying, he said just one sentence: "I have lived like an animal in the street, but I am going to die like an angel" … and he died beautifully.[36]

Mother Teresa extended mercy to that nameless man, and he radiated joy as a result. She believed that acts of mercy should also be bestowed upon the invisible among us — the children in their mothers' wombs:

And I feel one thing I want to share with you all, the greatest destroyer of peace today is the cry of the innocent unborn child. For if a mother can murder her own child in her own womb, what is left for you and for me to kill each other? Even in the scripture it is written: "Even if a mother could forget her child — I will not forget you — I have carved you in the palm of my hand." [Is 49:15-16][37]

As a pre-eminent peacemaker, Mother Teresa knew the critical importance of defending the lives of unborn children. Her prayer, issued so long ago in 1979, still resonates today:

Let us all pray that we have the courage to stand by the unborn child, and give the child an opportunity to love and to be loved, and I think with God's grace we will be able to bring peace into the world.[38]

SERVANT OF GOD DOROTHY DAY

I have often looked to the late Dorothy Day for inspiration because of her transformation from an individual without religious faith to a fervent Catholic. Day, an American journalist, had been enamored with prayer as a child, but abandoned the practice as she grew older. Day sought an abortion after learning of an unexpected pregnancy — a decision she would come to deeply regret.

By the time she gave birth to her daughter Tamar, Day had developed a renewed interest in faith — in particular, the Catholic faith. She wanted Tamar to be baptized, but she knew that the man she lived with was uninterested in religion. Indeed, their relationship ended as Day fully embraced Catholicism — not only for herself, but for her daughter.

She, along with a Frenchman named Peter Maurin, founded a newspaper called *The Catholic Worker*, which helped to spread Catholic thought and teaching to a wide audience. A few months before she died in 1980 — in what was, in a sense, her "Final Word" — Day wrote the following in the newspaper:

> We cannot love God unless we love each other, and to love we must know each

other. We know him in the breaking of bread, and we are not alone any more. Heaven is a banquet and life is a banquet, too, even with a crust, where there is companionship.

We have all known the long loneliness and we have learned that the only solution is love and that love comes with community.[39]

A community of love is our aim in the pro-life movement, which seeks to provide care and support for everyone from pregnant women facing dire circumstances to elderly individuals at risk of euthanasia.

In a 2015 speech before a joint session of Congress, Pope Francis explained how faith was the foundation of Day's good works:

Her social activism, her passion for justice and for the cause of the oppressed, were inspired by the Gospel, her faith, and the example of the saints.[40]

Day teaches us the critical importance of a caring heart as we go about our pro-life activism. We must recognize the fact that post-abortive women deserve healing and the hope which Divine Mercy can provide.

VENERABLE FULTON J. SHEEN

I was captivated when I first caught a glimpse of Archbishop Fulton J. Sheen on the Eternal Word Television Network. By then, the priest-philosopher had died, but his wit and wisdom lived on in reruns. With a dramatic flourish and good humor, Sheen communicated the truths of the Catholic faith in a signature style which I could not ignore.

Archbishop Sheen was a man made for the television age. His piercing eyes and infectious grin lit up the television screen and made people want to tune in during television's Golden Era of the 1950s and '60s. While I had missed watching Archbishop Sheen during his heyday, I found his message resonated with me long after he had passed from this earthly world.

"Holiness is like salt," the archbishop once stated. "Its usefulness to others must begin with self. As only the wise man can impart wisdom to others, so only the saintly can communicate sanctity. A man can bring forth to others only those treasures which he already has in his own heart."[41]

The television evangelist drew a distinct connection between abortion and euthanasia.

"We must also be careful if we give to mothers the right to destroy a child because it may have 'defective traits,' that someday a child may claim the right to destroy the mother because she has the 'destructive trait' of poverty or senility."[42]

Archbishop Sheen encouraged the faithful to "spiritually adopt" an unborn child in danger of abortion. He recommended that individuals pray each day for nine months for the successful delivery of the baby. The simple prayer is as powerful today as it was when he first composed it:

> Jesus, Mary, and Joseph; I love you very much, I beg you to spare the life of the unborn child that I have spiritually adopted; who is in danger of abortion.[43]

Archbishop Sheen also inspired the following quote from the late Illinois Congressman Henry Hyde, who authored the Hyde Amendment. This amendment, which bars federal taxpayer funding of abortion except in the rare cases of rape, incest, or to save the life of the mother, has been credited with saving the lives of more than 2.4 million people in the U.S.[44] Hyde said:

> When the time comes as it surely will, when we face that awesome moment, the final judgment, I've often thought, as Fulton Sheen wrote, that it is a terrible moment of loneliness. You have no advocates, you are there alone standing before God and a terror will rip through your soul like nothing you can imagine. But I really think that those in the pro-life movement will not be alone. I think there will be a chorus

of voices that have never been heard in this world but are heard beautifully and clearly in the next world and they will plead for anyone who has been in this movement. They will say to God, "Spare him because he loved us," and God will look at you and say not, "Did you succeed?" but "Did you try?"[45]

By following the example and heeding the words of spiritual mentors such as St. Teresa of Calcutta, Servant of God Dorothy Day, and Venerable Fulton J. Sheen, we can progress on the road to holiness and enhance our pro-life advocacy efforts.

Questions to Ponder

1. Who has served as a spiritual mentor to you in your life?

2. How can promoting the sanctity of human life also promote peace?

3. Have you ever abandoned an unhealthy relationship, such as Dorothy Day did, in order to pursue God?

4. Are you prepared to spiritually adopt a child this week?

Chapter 7

Acts of Mercy

"Pray with great confidence, with
confidence based upon the goodness
and infinite generosity of God and
upon the promises of Jesus Christ.
God is a spring of living water which
flows unceasingly into the hearts
of those who pray."

— Saint Louis de Montfort[46]

The pregnant woman was in desperate need — so desperate, in fact, that she had turned to strangers to assist her. She was six months pregnant when she lost her job because of the COVID-19 pandemic. The father of the baby then abandoned her. After that, she lost her housing, leaving her, her nine-year-old child, and her preborn baby with nowhere to go.

Her cry for help was not in vain. A network of volunteers paid for temporary housing, assisted her with her unemployment claim, and connected her with a nearby pregnancy resource center. A group of caring people then filled her online baby shower registry with enough goods to outfit an army of little ones.

A colleague of mine helped assemble the collection of items for the grateful mother. My co-worker was in awe of the outpouring of love for this woman who had previously felt abandoned and lost.[47]

This is the power of acts of mercy — they can be both life-changing and life-affirming. They are goodness in action — a testament to the love that God has bestowed on us and which we, in turn, share with others.

Action complements our prayers and allows people to see the face of Christ in us. It is much easier for them to believe in the living God when we serve them with a spirit of generosity.

Often, advocates for abortion ask where women will go, if abortion facilities shut their doors. It is up to us to check with the community of faith to see what resources are available in our local area. If they are insufficient, God may be calling us to help get local mothers' support groups and pregnancy care centers established.

Many opportunities exist to perform acts of mercy for pregnant women. Here are just a few:

- Host an in-person or online baby shower.

- Hold a diaper drive for a local pregnancy resource center.

- Distribute baby bottles at church and ask parishioners to return them filled with coins for your area pregnancy center.

- Offer to babysit so the woman can go to her OB/GYN appointments without toddlers in tow.

- Provide gift cards the woman can use at local supermarkets or department stores.

- Offer to clean the woman's house or do her grocery shopping while she rests.

- Serve as a "mentor mom" to a pregnant woman, guiding her through her pregnancy and parenting journey.

Also important is to extend a hand of hospitality to children and older people with disabilities. Sadly, in our throwaway culture, individuals with disabilities are often considered expendable. A case in point is the tragic statistic that an estimated 67 percent of preborn babies diagnosed with Down syndrome are aborted.[48]

By performing acts of mercy for people with disabilities, we can help to establish a welcoming culture that demonstrates the love of Christ. As Jesus says to the righteous when the Son of Man comes at the end of the age in Matthew 25:35-36:

> For I was hungry and you gave me food,
> I was thirsty and you gave me drink, a
> stranger and you welcomed me, naked and
> you clothed me, ill and you cared for me,
> in prison and you visited me.

Those advanced in age could also use the touch of love that an act of mercy can provide. Research indicates that people who seek "assisted suicide" often do so because of feelings of loneliness and isolation. They search for doctors who will write them prescriptions for lethal doses of drugs, when what they could really use is the support that comes from friendship. Indeed, the antidote to the anti-life culture is love.

An act of mercy for an older person can be as simple as taking him or her to the grocery store, shoveling the snow off the sidewalk, or mowing the lawn. Simple acts can convey to an elderly man or woman the special place he or she holds in God's eyes.

As Mother Teresa stated, "Not all of us can do great things, but we can do small things with great love."[49]

 Questions to Ponder

1. What acts of mercy have you been the recipient of in the last month?

2. What acts of mercy could you perform for a pregnant woman this week?

3. Is there a person with a disability in your life whom you could help?

4. Which older person in your life could use an act of mercy this week?

Chapter 8

Merciful Awakenings

"So whoever is in Christ is a new creation:
the old things have passed away; behold,
new things have come. And all this is from
God, who has reconciled us to himself
through Christ and given us the ministry of
reconciliation, namely, God was reconciling
the world to himself in Christ, not counting
their trespasses against them and entrust-
ing to us the message of reconciliation. So
we are ambassadors for Christ, as if God
were appealing through us. We implore you
on behalf of Christ, be reconciled to God."

— 2 Corinthians 5:17-20

Our God is a God of second chances. This is crit-
ically important to remember as we go about
the work of renewing a culture of life. The most
stalwart defenders of abortion can have a change of
heart and embrace the pro-life cause. Such transfor-
mations have happened time and time again among
abortionists, abortion center directors, and abortion
facility staff members.

The phenomenon has even occurred in the political sphere, where one-time apologists for the abortion industry have become pro-life public officials. For instance, as Governor of California, Ronald Reagan signed a law legalizing abortion in 1967.[50] He regretted the action and became a staunch defender of innocent human life as President in the 1980s. Such conversions have also occurred in the area of arts and the media (I can attest to this firsthand as a self-described "pro-choice" reporter who is living her "second act" as a pro-life activist).

This is why we must be gentle in our efforts to evangelize about the pro-life cause. We must strive to be non-judgmental as we go about the business of rebuilding a society which embraces rather than erases life. We must keep in mind that today's anti-life activist could become tomorrow's pro-life champion.

We need only look to Scripture for historical evidence of such conversions. Consider, for instance, the case of Saul, a tormenter and persecutor of Christians who did an about-face and became the eloquent Apostle Paul:

> On that journey as I drew near to Damascus, about noon a great light from the sky suddenly shone around me. I fell to the ground and heard a voice saying to me, "Saul, Saul, why are you persecuting Me?"

I replied, "Who are you, sir? And he said to me, "I am Jesus the Nazorean whom you are persecuting." My companions saw the light but did not hear the voice of the one who spoke to me.

I asked, "What shall I do, sir?" The Lord answered me, "Get up and go into Damascus, and there you will be told about everything appointed for you to do."[51]

A disciple named Ananias subsequently answered the call of the Lord to lay hands on Saul and help him regain his sight. Ananias said:

"Saul, my brother, regain your sight." And at that very moment I regained my sight and saw him. Then he said, "The God of our ancestors designated you to know his will, to see the Righteous One, and to hear the sound of his voice; for you will be his witness before all to what you have seen and heard.

"Now, why delay? Get up and have yourself baptized and your sins washed away, calling upon his name."[52]

Mary Magdalene is another Biblical figure who received a merciful awakening. Recall how she became a follower of Jesus:

Afterward he journeyed from one town and village to another, preaching and

proclaiming the good news of the king-
dom of God. Accompanying him were
the Twelve and some women who had
been cured of evil spirits and infirmities,
Mary, called Magdalene, from whom seven
demons had gone out … [53]

Mary Magdalene later received the honor of seeing
Jesus after He had risen from the dead:

When he had risen, early on the first day
of the week, he appeared first to Mary
Magdalene, out of whom he had driven
seven demons. She went and told his
companions who were mourning and
weeping.[54]

So many who now labor in the vineyards of the
pro-life movement had to have the "scales fall from
their eyes" before they recognized that abortion is
the taking of an innocent human life. I am reminded
of former Planned Parenthood center director
Abby Johnson, whose life story forms the basis of
the movie "Unplanned." It was only after viewing
an ultrasound-guided abortion and witnessing the
destruction of the unborn child that Abby felt com-
pelled to leave the abortion industry.[55]

A similar situation occurred years earlier when
Dr. Bernard Nathanson, one of the founders of the
abortion lobbying group known as NARAL, became
convinced of the humanity of the unborn baby as

a result of ultrasound imaging. As Dr. Nathanson, maker of the film "The Silent Scream," stated:

> Mothers and fathers for the first time have been afforded a view of their unborn child by these spectacular technologies. And those machines that we now use every day, have convinced us that beyond question the unborn child is simply another human being, another member of the human community … indistinguishable in every way from any of us."[56]

When I was a reporter, I recall the leader of a local pro-life group sending me a hand-written note following one of my radio reports. The note was kind and merciful, and I kept it in my desk drawer for a long time as a reminder of my pro-life roots. I believe that little pink note had a hand in my ultimate conversion to the pro-life cause.

Questions to Ponder

1. Have you ever experienced a "Road to Damascus" moment?

2. To what extent can you relate to Mary Magdalene's story of healing and hope?

3. Have you ever considered "spiritually adopting" an abortion industry worker?

4. Would you consider writing a note to a media professional, encouraging him or her to seek the truth about abortion or another pro-life issue?

Chapter 9

Words of Mercy

"Speak to the world about My mercy; let all mankind recognize My unfathomable mercy."

— Jesus, speaking to St. Faustina[57]

Every few weeks, I hear the words of comfort that come with Confession. After I have named my sins, the priest soothes my soul with the prayer of absolution:

> God the Father of mercies, through the death and resurrection of His Son has reconciled the world to himself and sent the Holy Spirit among us for the forgiveness of sins; through the ministry of the Church may God give you pardon and peace, and I absolve you from your sins in the name of the Father, and of the Son, and of the Holy Spirit. Amen.[58]

In a broken world and in the midst of my own brokenness, God reaches into my life and showers me with His abundant grace. I am unworthy of this gift, and yet the Lord bestows it with love. The priest's words assure me of God's forgiveness and offer me the peace which surpasses all understanding.

In our social media-driven world, words of mercy can be difficult to come by. Fueled by anger, frustration, and the bravura that can come from hiding behind an electronic screen, people routinely spew out venomous verbal attacks.

When the topic of discussion is abortion, the vitriol can arise like a geyser. At times, the diatribes may stem from post-abortion trauma; a woman or man who has suffered the loss of a child through abortion experiences a profound pain which manifests itself in anger toward pro-life advocates.

In circumstances such as these, it becomes all the more important for us to heed the words of our Lord Jesus Christ: "When someone strikes you on [your] right cheek, turn the other one to him as well."[59]

It can be challenging to issue words of mercy, especially during times of confrontation. Again, Scripture can be our guide in this regard:

> Conduct yourselves wisely toward outsiders, making the most of the opportunity. Let your speech always be gracious, seasoned with salt, so that you know how you should respond to each one.[60]

On a human level, consistently engaging in merciful speech can seem daunting. That is why we need to turn to our Lord in continual prayer.

One prayer I have found especially helpful is the "Prayer to Be Merciful to Others." Whether we recite it as a Morning Offering or a nightly Examination of Conscience, it can be highly beneficial in helping us to tame our tongues:

O Most Holy Trinity! As many times as I breathe, as many times as my heart beats, as many times as my blood pulsates through my body, so many thousand times do I want to glorify Your mercy.

I want to be completely transformed into Your mercy and to be Your living reflection, O Lord. May the greatest of all divine attributes, that of Your unfathomable mercy, pass through my heart and soul to my neighbor.

Help me, O Lord, that my eyes may be merciful, so that I may never suspect or judge from appearances, but look for what is beautiful in my neighbors' souls and come to their rescue.

Help me, that my ears may be merciful, so that I may give heed to my neighbors' needs and not be indifferent to their pains and moanings.

Help me, O Lord, that my tongue may be merciful, so that I should never speak negatively of my neighbor, but have a word of comfort and forgiveness for all.

Help me, O Lord, that my hands may be merciful and filled with good deeds, so that I may do only good to my neighbors and take upon myself the more difficult and toilsome tasks.

Help me, that my feet may be merciful, so that I may hurry to assist my neighbor, overcoming my own fatigue and weariness. My true rest is in the service of my neighbor.

Help me, O Lord, that my heart may be merciful so that I myself may feel all the sufferings of my neighbor. I will refuse my heart to no one. I will be sincere even with those who, I know, will abuse my kindness. And I will lock myself up in the most merciful Heart of Jesus. I will bear my own suffering in silence. May Your mercy, O Lord, rest upon me.

You Yourself command me to exercise the three degrees of mercy. The first: the act of mercy, of whatever kind. The second: the word of mercy — if I cannot carry out a work of mercy, I will assist by my words. The third: prayer — if I cannot show mercy by deeds or words, I can always do so by prayer. My prayer reaches out even there where I cannot reach out physically.

O my Jesus, transform me into Yourself, for You can do all things.[61]

Words of mercy are especially valuable as we work to promote the pro-life cause. It is difficult to be persuasive if our speech is condescending and judgemental. We should remember that we are all sinners dependent on God's mercy for our very survival.

When we broach an emotion-tinged topic such as abortion, we should recall the tenderness with which Jesus addressed the Samaritan woman at the well:

Jesus said to her, "Give me a drink."

His disciples had gone into the town to buy food.

The Samaritan woman said to him, "How can you, a Jew, ask me, a Samaritan woman, for a drink?" (For Jews use nothing in common with Samaritans.)

Jesus answered and said to her, "If you knew the gift of God and who is saying to you, 'Give me a drink,' you would have asked him and he would have given you living water."

[The woman] said to him, "Sir, you do not even have a bucket and the well is deep; where then can you get this living water? Are you greater than our father Jacob, who gave us this well and drank from it himself with his children and his flocks?"

Jesus answered and said to her, "Everyone who drinks this water will be thirsty again; but whoever drinks the water I shall give will never thirst; the water I shall give will become in him a spring of water welling up to eternal life."[62]

In championing the cause of life, we are offering people a better approach to resolving the many issues that confront us. Abortion does not solve poverty, homelessness, academic troubles, or relationship problems — it only creates a host of new problems. Neither does euthanasia solve medical issues such as severe depression or intense physical pain. We need to speak life into these situations by offering life-affirming solutions such as psychological counseling, enhanced medical care, and palliative care.

Our words of mercy can open doors of opportunity and hope to those who are struggling. They can act as a healing balm which can help to save lives.

Questions to Ponder

1. Do you need to change your approach to social media in order to make it more compassionate toward pregnant women in crisis situations?

2. How has the Sacrament of Reconciliation informed your views about mercy?

3. What can you do to add more words of mercy to your daily speech?

4. How does the story of the woman at the well give you hope for the future?

Chapter 10

A Sinner's Guide to Divine Mercy

"Those who sincerely say 'Jesus, I trust in You' will find comfort in all their anxieties and fears. There is nothing that man needs more than Divine Mercy — that love which is benevolent, which is compassionate, which raises man above his weakness to the infinite heights of the holiness of God."

— Pope St. John Paul II[63]

During an especially dark time of my life, I felt as if I were beyond God's mercy. I had gone to Confession again and again — and yet, I was on the brink of despair for my immortal soul. I believed — falsely — that God's love no longer applied to me. I felt adrift on a sea of desperation and I could not imagine the Lord sending me a "rescue boat."

But He did — and it was manned by a kindly young priest who understood my pain and wanted me to understand that God could save me from it. He stressed to me the efficacy of the Sacrament of Reconciliation — that with a sincere confession,

I could be assured of the good Lord's forgiveness. Eventually I came to understand the truth of his words and realized that all was not lost. It was a powerful moment of grace for which I am forever grateful.

Perhaps, like me, you wrestle with the concept of Divine Mercy. As incredible as it sounds, God is eager to bestow His mercy upon us. Divine Mercy has been referred to as "the greatest grassroots movement in the history of the Catholic Church."[64] It is an amazing reflection of the infinite love of God, poured out upon His people.

In our suffering and sinfulness, God shows His endless compassion for us. Divine Mercy is not something we earn, but a form of love that the Lord freely gives to us. It can be said that every good thing in our lives is a manifestation of God's mercy. Divine Mercy is the good news reflected in the Gospel — and shared through the message disseminated by the 20th century mystic known as St. Maria Faustina Kowalska.

Jesus revealed to St. Faustina the importance of observing the Sunday after Easter as the Feast of Divine Mercy. As He said to the beloved saint, **"The soul that will go to Confession and receive Holy Communion shall obtain complete forgiveness of sins and punishment."**[65] Father Michael Gaitley, MIC explains the significance of Jesus' words:

It means that if we were to die right after receiving this grace, then we wouldn't have to go to purgatory! In other words, our slate is wiped clean.[66]

What an extraordinary grace the Lord offers on Divine Mercy Sunday! The feast allows us to begin again — to embark on a path forward without having to drag our sins along. As a result, it is a most powerful sign of God's abiding love for us.

We can also receive wondrous blessings just by gazing upon the Image of Divine Mercy. This Image depicts Jesus with His right hand raised to bless us. Two light rays shine from His Sacred Heart. The red ray and the pale ray signify the Blood and water which emerged from His side as He hung on the Cross at His Crucifixion. The image is accompanied by the simple prayer: "Jesus, I trust in You."

If you struggle with your own image of God — unable to view Him as all-loving — the Divine Mercy image can help you to shift your perspective. As Fr. Gaitley explains:

> One grace that comes through the Image is this: It heals the way people often mistakenly view God. Here's what we mean. People too often have a false image of God. They're afraid of Him and see Him as some mean ogre just out to ruin their fun. Well, the Image of Divine Mercy

helps to change that. In it, we discover our Merciful Savior Who surely calls us to conversion but Who also blesses us, loves us, and is deserving of all of our trust.[67]

We can, in turn, show our love for Jesus by observing the Hour of Divine Mercy at 3 o'clock in the afternoon. It's a wonderful time to pray the Divine Mercy Chaplet for the souls of those who die that day.

In case you are not familiar with it (and I only learned of it as an adult), the Chaplet is prayed on Rosary beads. It begins with an Our Father, a Hail Mary, and the Apostle's Creed. On the five large beads of the Rosary we pray, "Eternal Father, I offer You the Body and Blood, Soul and Divinity of Your dearly beloved Son, our Lord Jesus Christ, in atonement for our sins and those of the whole world." On each of the smaller beads of each decade, we pray, "For the sake of His sorrowful Passion, have mercy on us and on the whole world."

As the Lord said to St. Faustina:

When this chaplet is said by the bedside of a dying person ... unfathomable mercy envelops the soul, and the very depths of My tender mercy are moved for the sake of the sorrowful Passion of My Son.[68]

Another awe-inspiring devotion is the Divine Mercy Novena. The Novena can be prayed at any time, but it customarily begins on Good Friday and continues for nine days. This prayer demonstrates the exceptional breadth of Divine Mercy, as each day is devoted to a different intention. These intentions include: sinners, priests and religious, people who do not believe in God, little children, the Holy Souls in Purgatory, and souls who are lukewarm, among other needs.[69]

Observing the Divine Mercy devotions and sharing them with others can help us, the wounded healers, to reach out to others with mercy. At a time when sin abounds, grace is also plentiful. It is with this abundant grace that we can heal the divisions within our world that keep us from fully embracing the life-giving Gospel.

Questions to Ponder

1. In what ways is it apparent to you that Divine Mercy is really all that we need?

2. Have you ever felt beyond God's mercy? What gave you hope during that difficult time?

3. Does your image of God need healing? Why or why not?

4. How can you observe the Hour of Mercy this week?

Chapter 11

Pro-Life 101

"I am happy to die because I have lived my life without wasting a minute on those things which do not please God."

— Blessed Carlo Acutis[70]

M y journey to the pro-life movement was both spiritual and practical. A daily Rosary helped to open my heart to the humanity of the unborn child. Books awakened me to the development of the child in the womb. I had to be spiritually ready to embrace the most vulnerable, but I also needed some basic tools in order to be able to advocate on their behalf.

If you are new to the pro-life cause, the following information will be helpful in your formation to become an ambassador for life. If you are a veteran pro-lifer, the following facts will serve as a helpful refresher course. For the most up-to-date pro-life information, I recommend an online source such as National Right to Life's website: www.nrlc.org. There, you will find the latest statistics, key legislative updates, and other useful material for your defense of the voiceless among us.

The *Catechism of the Catholic Church* makes it clear — abortion violates the Fifth Commandment's exhortation not to kill:

> Formal cooperation in an abortion constitutes a grave offense. The Church attaches the canonical penalty of excommunication to this crime against human life.[71]

With a sincere confession, an individual involved in the crime of abortion can seek forgiveness from God. It is especially important to communicate this truth to women who have lost a child to abortion. As the *Catechism* also points out:

> The Church does not thereby intend to restrict the scope of mercy. Rather, she makes clear the gravity of the crime committed, the irreparable harm done to the innocent who is put to death, as well as to the parents and the whole of society.[72]

As of this writing, nearly a million abortions occur each year in the U.S. — a staggering figure by any measurement.[73] Tragically, more than 63 million abortions have taken place in the U.S. since the 1973 Supreme Court ruling *Roe v. Wade* and its companion case, *Doe v. Bolton*, which legalized abortion across the country.[74]

"In its twin *Roe v. Wade* and *Doe v. Bolton* decisions, which were handed down on January 22, 1973, the Court legalized abortion for any reason,"

National Right to Life Committee President Carol Tobias has written.[75]

According to the Charlotte Lozier Institute, by just eight weeks after conception, the preborn child can move his hands together. As the Institute notes on its website, "The embryo can also roll over within the amniotic sac, squint, grasp and point his toes."[76]

The abortion industry itself reports that the majority of abortions are obtained by women who already had at least one child.[77] Moreover, African-Americans represent a disproportionate number of those obtaining abortions, giving rise to what some Black leaders have described as a black genocide.[78] Prominent African-American leader Pastor Clenard Childress has said, "The most dangerous place for an African-American is in the womb."[79]

Surgical abortions, in which precious preborn babies are suctioned out of their mothers' wombs in suction curettage procedures, or torn limb-by-limb through dismemberment abortions, are inherently violent acts. Increasingly, abortions are performed chemically through use of the abortion pill. This is actually a two-pill process, where the first pill kills the baby and the second pill, taken six to 48 hours later, causes the mother to expel the baby.[80]

The good news is that, if a woman changes her mind after taking the first abortion pill, she may be able to halt the abortion process through the use of the natural hormone progesterone. This is a process known as Abortion Pill Reversal (APR). Research shows that the reversal protocol has successfully saved pregnancies in 64 percent of the women who have undergone the APR process.[81] By contacting a pro-life OB/GYN, the woman has a chance to save her baby from death. To learn more about the miraculous practice of Abortion Pill Reversal, please visit AbortionPillReversal.com.

Women can also obtain comprehensive counseling and material assistance during their pregnancies through some 3,000 pregnancy support centers throughout the U.S.[82] These life-affirming centers, which do not refer for abortions, offer everything from diapers to day-care referrals, and from maternity clothes to mentoring. All of their services are offered free to their thousands of clients.

Meanwhile, human life also is being threatened increasingly by the twin threats of assisted suicide and euthanasia. Assisted suicide, also known as doctor-prescribed suicide, involves a physician prescribing a lethal dose of drugs to a patient who requests it. Euthanasia is deliberately ending a person's life under the guise of relieving suffering.

The Patients' Rights Action Fund, which lobbies against laws permitting assisted suicide, notes that less than five percent of individuals who died by assisted suicide were referred for psychiatric evaluation. And yet, research indicates at least a quarter of those persons who seek assisted suicide are suffering from depression, anxiety, or another psychological illness.[83]

In addition, there have been numerous cases in which a patient initially sought assisted suicide but, as a result of receiving wise counsel from a pro-life physician, embraced life instead. Enhanced palliative care has also been shown to reduce the likelihood of assisted suicide.

It is important to note that hope for salvation still exists for those who die by suicide. As Fr. Chris Alar, MIC, and Jason Lewis, MIC, point out in their book, *After Suicide: There's Hope for Them and for You* (Marian Press, 2019):

> The *Catechism* addresses this question directly, saying, "Grave psychological disturbances, anguish, or grave fear of hardship, suffering, or torture can diminish the responsibility of the one committing suicide" (2282). Read that again. Please, read and reread this declaration of Mother Church. Let it sink into your heart, as if coming from the lips of a tender, loving, and understanding mother. Our beloved's culpability, the responsibility for their action, may be reduced if they experienced "grave psychological disturbances, anguish, or grave fear of hardship, suffering, or torture." In the case of suicide, one could

even argue that "torture" could apply to mental, not just physical, duress.[84]

The *Catechism of the Catholic Church* also has much to say about the deadly danger of euthanasia:

> Those whose lives are diminished or weakened deserve special respect. Sick or handicapped persons should be helped to lead lives as normal as possible.
>
> Whatever its motives and means, direct euthanasia consists in putting an end to the lives of handicapped, sick, or dying persons. It is morally unacceptable.[85]

Assisted suicide and euthanasia should not be confused with the legitimate cessation of extraordinary life-saving measures that would be overly burdensome to a dying person:

> Discontinuing medical procedures that are burdensome, dangerous, extraordinary, or disproportionate to the expected outcome can be legitimate; it is the refusal of "over-zealous" treatment. Here one does not will to cause death; one's inability to impede it is merely accepted. The decisions should be made by the patient if he is competent and able or, if not, by those legally entitled to act for the patient, whose reasonable will and legitimate interests must always be respected.[86]

As pro-life advocates, we need to be in a continual mode of educating ourselves. As flight attendants direct adult passengers to place their oxygen masks over their own faces before they attempt to help a child, so we must learn the fundamentals of preserving life before we can pass them on to the next generation. Thankfully, with the internet, an abundance of trustworthy pro-life resources are just a few clicks away.

Questions to Ponder

1. Were you aware of the vast number of abortions that have taken place in the U.S.? Is there someone in your sphere of influence who also needs to know this information?

2. Did you know about Abortion Pill Reversal? Is there someone you can share that information with this week?

3. How can the so-called "right to die" become "the duty to die"?

4. What one step can you take this week to become better educated on the pro-life issue?

Chapter 12

Feminine Genius

"Thank you, *every woman,* for the simple fact of being *a woman!* Through the insight which is so much a part of your womanhood you enrich the world's understanding and help to make human relations more honest and authentic."

— Pope St. John Paul II[87]

Pope St. John Paul II recognized a unique feminine genius which characterizes the women of our world. In his 1995 "Letter to Women," the Holy Father expressed gratitude for women and the various roles they play in society.

The 21st century saint was particularly grateful for mothers, who demonstrate compassion and love to the young children in our midst:

> Thank you, *women who are mothers!* You have sheltered human beings within yourselves in a unique experience of joy and travail. This experience makes you become God's own smile upon the newborn child, the one who guides your child's first steps,

who helps it to grow, and who is the anchor as the child makes its way along the journey of life.[88]

Pope John Paul also saw the benefits of women using their feminine genius to advance progress in the affairs of the world:

> Thank you, *women who work!* You are present and active in every area of life — social, economic, cultural, artistic and political. In this way you make an indispensable contribution to the growth of a culture which unites reason and feeling, to a model of life ever open to the sense of "mystery", to the establishment of economic and political structures ever more worthy of humanity.[89]

The Pontiff also praised women for the singular contribution they can make in addressing society's problems, from quality of life to euthanasia:

> In all these areas a greater presence of women in society will prove most valuable, for it will help to manifest the contradictions present when society is organized solely according to the criteria of efficiency and productivity, and it will force systems to be redesigned in a way which favors the processes of humanization which mark the "civilization of love."[90]

Moreover, in his 1988 Apostolic Letter entitled *Mulieris Dignitatem* (*The Dignity and Vocation of Women*), Pope John Paul expressed gratitude for evidence of feminine genius through the ages:

> The Church gives thanks *for all the manifestations of the feminine "genius"* which have appeared in the course of history, in the midst of all peoples and nations; she gives thanks for all the charisms which the Holy Spirit distributes to women in the history of the People of God, for all the victories which she owes to their faith, hope and charity: she gives thanks for all *the fruits of feminine holiness.*[91]

When women tap into their feminine genius as biological mothers, adoptive mothers, and spiritual mothers, they can contribute mightily to the renewal of a culture of life. Their nurturing and careful attention to the needs of people helps to promote the civilization of love of which the Holy Father wrote.

Notice, too, that Pope John Paul mentioned the fruits of feminine holiness. The more that women aspire to holiness, the greater the possibility of unleashing the feminine genius. Such holiness can be nurtured through frequent prayer, reception of the Sacraments, and spiritual reading.

It can also be quite helpful to have like-minded (and like-spirited) women join together on the journey of holiness. These associations can take the form of Bible studies and other spiritual enrichment programs; Rosary groups; or other lay-inspired movements in the Church such as the Legion of Mary and Cursillo.

Whenever women come together to share their faith, wondrous things can happen. I have seen the prayers of a committed group of women open doors to employment that seemed to be locked shut ... lead premature babies to the road to wholeness and health ... and ease the transition of older relatives in the last stages of earthly life.

I am reminded of the two sisters who befriended Jesus — Mary and Martha. Mary was known for sitting at Jesus' feet, listening to Him teach, while Martha was busy about the running of the household. Martha's attention to housekeeping details was obsessive — so much so that she missed the joy that Mary experienced in rapt attention before Christ.

The quiet contemplation which can mark the "Mary" side of a woman's nature can combine with the hospitality that distinguishes her "Martha" side, helping to build up a loving community in the Church and beyond it. Indeed, the feminine genius flourishes when women adopt the "best practices" of Mary and Martha.

The pro-abortion culture has done a tremendous disservice to women, telling them that an unborn child's life is just a matter of a woman's "choice." Women can be haunted for years by their decision to abort a child. I recall a woman in her 80s who called a pro-life office, weeping over the loss of her baby from a long-ago abortion. Rather than an act of liberation, the abortion kept her emotionally imprisoned, unable to break free on her own.

In such cases, the mercy of God can break through the invisible chains, allowing the woman to experience a new freedom in Christ. Spiritual mothers can lead such a woman onto the path of healing through their prayers and compassionate response.

Questions to Ponder

1. To what extent have you observed or experienced "feminine genius?"

2. In what ways can feminine genius build up your family? The Church?

3. Can you see aspects of Mary and Martha in your personality or the personality of a woman you love?

4. What concrete way can you assist a woman who is hurting this week?

Chapter 13

A Man's Perspective

"The Cross is the school of love."

— Saint Maximilian Kolbe[92]

I recall the image as if it were yesterday — the delicate, stick-like legs and arms, the tiny head that distinguished my premature baby sister. She spent her first days of life on earth in an incubator, and our parents were not sure she would make it. But, with the tenacity that would become her hallmark, she not only survived, she thrived, under the loving care of my mother and father.

My father was a gentle soul who exuded a quiet strength that made him our valiant protector. He had served in the Korean Conflict, and he had a soldier's dedication to duty. I recall that when he died many decades later, it seemed as if the world was less safe with him gone.

My baby sister and I were so privileged to grow up with a father who mirrored God's love to us. He was an encourager who always served as our biggest cheerleader. With his wind beneath our wings, we knew we could soar.

While the world may try to portray abortion as entirely a "woman's issue," it is equally important for men to play a role in rebuilding a culture of life. We need them to serve as models of St. Joseph, serving as the backbone of our families. They can provide the steadfast love which complements a mother's affection for a child.

Sadly, men often play a role in a woman's decision to abort a child, as noted by Kevin Burke, associate director of Rachel's Vineyard Ministries, a healing ministry for those who have been involved in abortion.

"The majority of men encourage, manipulate and even force their girlfriends, partners or wives to abort," Burke told the *Zenit International News Agency*.[93]

Men may also abandon the child's mother when they learn of her pregnancy. Burke continued:

> An important part of healing for many men begins with an agonizing repentance of their role in the abortion procedure and the failure to protect mother and baby from harm. This act of humility opens the door for them to acknowledge that they have also lost a son or a daughter.[94]

Vincent Rue, the co-director for the Institute for Pregnancy Loss and expert on post-abortion trauma, cites nearly 30 studies that help to gauge men's reactions to abortion trauma. "In one study, most men felt overwhelmed, with many experiencing disturbing thoughts of the abortion (Shostak & McLouth, 1984)."[95] Men may be reluctant to articulate their grief, going silent or expressing feelings of hostility.

In another study, Rue points out abortion's effects on men's relationships. Men tend to try to cope alone while experiencing a despair which may be even greater than that experienced by women following abortion.

This situation makes it all the more important for men to reach out to one another with brotherly love. A man can help guide his friend to a Rachel's Vineyard retreat, where that friend can receive compassionate understanding and healing.

It has been said that the best response to an unexpected pregnancy is an individual willing to say to a pregnant woman: How can I help? This is all the more true for the father of the child. While a man willing to step in and assume the role of father might not always receive a warm welcome from the mother of the child, he can often be the determinative factor in a decision not to seek abortion.

If a man is willing to accompany the mother of his preborn child to a pregnancy resource center where she can see an ultrasound image of her baby, she is far more likely to choose life for her child. Fraternal groups such as the Knights of Columbus have led the way in donating money for ultrasound machines for use in pregnancy help centers. The Knights report as many as 80 percent of women will opt for life for their babies after viewing an ultrasound image of the child in utero.[96]

Fathers of aborted children who regret the abortions are part of a movement called the Silent No More Awareness Campaign. You can read their testimonies at SilentNoMoreAwareness.org. Among them is Jon, who offered his story of hope and healing at the 2022 March for Life:

> If our story can save someone else from having an abortion, that would be so great. Because, to this day, I still wonder what kind of person our child would have been. That is why we are Silent No More.[97]

Another man, Scott, offered his moving testimony at the 2019 March for Life in Ottawa, Canada:

> I turned to alcohol to deal with the emotional complications of my guilt, anger and loss, but it didn't help. I eventually went to a priest and confessed my sin of abortion involvement to him, and he reassured me of God's forgiveness. As time went on, I found more healing through helping fatherless children.[98]

Meanwhile, David, also from Canada, found peace after he experienced healing following his devastating experiences with abortion:

My recovery from the abortions began with taking responsibility for the gravity of what I did. I received counseling, and went on many retreats including Rachel's Vineyard.[99]

As these testimonies demonstrate, many men have suffered greatly as a result of abortion culture. Thanks to the healing power of mercy, men who were involved in an abortion and who now regret their role can be powerful allies in the effort to re-establish a culture of life.

Questions to Ponder

1. What men have you known who have mirrored the love of God the Father and St. Joseph?

2. Would you consider praying for a man who is grieving the loss of a child to abortion?

3. What do you think has been the impact of "lost fatherhood" on our society?

4. What action could you take this week to assist a father under stress?

Chapter 14

Legacy of Love

"Go out into the world today and love the people you meet. Let your presence light new light in the hearts of people."

— Saint Teresa of Calcutta[100]

Mother Teresa began her religious life as a teacher. She had a heart for teaching and a heart for the family and believed that loving one's family was essential for bringing peace into the world.

Part of loving one's family is sharing our values with them. That includes our pro-life principles, which are an extension of our faith. As we cannot wait years to water a plant and expect it to grow healthy and strong, we cannot delay passing on our pro-life beliefs to our children and grandchildren. We have to begin early to instill in them a profound respect for human life.

Fortunately, opportunities for such teaching abound in our 21st century world. For instance, we should freely share ultrasound images of preborn babies with our children and grandchildren. They should be able to recognize the humanity of the baby in the womb. If your own family is not blessed with ultrasound images, consider accessing them on the Internet. A quick search of the World Wide Web will yield an abundance of images you can share with the youngest members of your family.

A number of pro-life organizations, such as the Pennsylvania Pro-Life Federation and its local county-based chapters, also have sets of "soft touch" fetal models available to borrow. These life-like models depict the preborn baby at various stages of development. They are realistic in size and weight and can serve as a great teaching tool.

Another helpful practice is for your family to spiritually adopt an unborn baby. This simple act of love requires you to pray each day for the health and safety of an unborn child over a period of nine months. If you do not know a child to pray for, you can just ask God to direct your prayers to the child most in need. Who knows how many precious lives you can save through these heartfelt prayers?

In recent years, a number of picture books have emerged which seek to instill pro-life values in the young. These beautifully-illustrated books showcase the unborn child in an age-appropriate way for young readers. You can consult your local right-to-life organization or pregnancy resource center for a list of titles.

If you can engage in family-oriented pro-life activities, it can help to convince your children and/or grandchildren of the rightness of the pro-life cause.

These activities can run the gamut — from shopping for diapers for a family in need to volunteering to sort baby clothes at a local pregnancy resource center. Your family might also consider taking part in a weekly Holy Hour for the intention of conversions to the pro-life movement. By engaging in family activities, you are helping to make memories that will last long after your children and/or grandchildren are grown.

Yet another way to pass on a pro-life legacy is to take advantage of teachable moments. If there is a pregnancy in your family, you might want to invest in a phone app such as "Sprout." This provides timely reminders of the growth of the preborn child throughout a mother's pregnancy. Sharing these reminders can become a wonderful bonding experience for the whole family.

In addition, do not neglect praying for your loved ones to embrace the pro-life cause. Prayers can open up windows of opportunities for learning that might not exist otherwise. It is never too soon to pray for your children and grandchildren to embrace pro-life principles. From a young age, they are immersed in a culture which all too often abandons vulnerable pre-born children, people with disabilities, and the frail elderly.

Moreover, it can be argued that pro-life beliefs are more likely to be "caught" than taught. If children see you caring for both the very young and the very old with tenderness and affection, they are likely to emulate what they see. The more we live out our pro-life values, the greater the legacy we are likely to leave for our descendants.

But what if your children grow up to abandon the pro-life cause? What then? The most important thing is to continue to love your children unconditionally, and to communicate that love to them on a regular basis. It can also be helpful to ask them questions about why they believe what they do. Through such caring conversations, you might be able to clear up any misunderstandings that your loved ones have about abortion, euthanasia, and other pro-life issues.

You may find yourself in the position of St. Monica, who prayed for years for the conversion of her son, whom we know as St. Augustine of Hippo.

As God never gives up on us, so we can never give up on our loved ones. The Lord can open up doors to understanding, helping our children and grandchildren to find and, ultimately, to embrace the truth.

Questions to Ponder

1. What "teachable moments" exist right now to share your pro-life beliefs with the younger members of your family?

2. What may be holding you back from talking pro-life with your children and/or grandchildren?

3. Are you reluctant to speak about pro-life issues? Why or why not?

4. What one thing can you do this week to demonstrate the sanctity of life to the younger generation?

Chapter 15

Culture of Caring

"And do not be afraid to participate in
the revolution to which He calls you:
the revolution of tenderness."

— Pope Francis[101]

Pope Francis has invited both young and old alike to become part of a revolution of tenderness. This is in direct contrast to the harshness that seems to permeate the modern world. So often, we see where violence begets violence and hatred leads to more hatred. Such a society can have a dehumanizing effect, where individuals fail to see one another as brothers and sisters.

But a tender culture is a loving culture, one that recognizes the extraordinary gift that each human life represents. The more we tap into our tenderness, the more love we can unleash in our families, in our communities, and in our country.

The Holy Father has defined tenderness as "the love that comes close and becomes real. It is a movement that starts from our heart and reaches the eyes, the ears, and the hands."[102]

Think about that concept for a moment. Tenderness is not a love in theory, but a love in action. It has a depth and breadth which makes it concrete. It finds its expression in the way we look at people … the manner in which we listen to them … and the comforting touch we give them. It is a love which begins in the heart and transfigures us so that we become another Christ to others.

I am reminded of the definition of love offered in 1 Corinthians 13:4-8:

> Love is patient, love is kind. It is not jealous, [love] is not pompous, it is not inflated, it is not rude, it does not seek its own interests, it is not quick-tempered, it does not brood over injury, it does not rejoice over wrongdoing but rejoices with the truth. It bears all things, believes all things, hopes all things, endures all things. Love never fails.

This Scripture reading has become a hallmark of weddings, which is understandable. After all, it provides the kind of road map that can lead to a happy married life. But it can also be applicable to our efforts to renew a culture of life. Such a culture will be patient, kind, and cooperative. It will be the opposite of quick-tempered and brooding, and it will indeed rejoice with the truth: that life is a good that should be nurtured and protected. In renewing a culture of life, we seek to establish a civilization of love, a culture of caring.

An integral part of re-establishing a culture which respects life is electing public officials who are willing to safeguard the innocent through legislation and executive action. Civic engagement and voting are critical aspects of rebuilding our society. We need to partner with elected office-holders in promoting life-affirming policies that will lead to the culture of caring that we long for.

But you do not have to be an elected official to make a difference. The worldwide Cursillo movement speaks of evangelizing within a square meter of one's own body. I once saw a member of Cursillo demonstrate that idea by taking a Hula-Hoop and placing it around his waist. Whenever someone touched the hoop, that individual was a recipient of his evangelization efforts. In other words, we are called to spread the love of Christ to everyone with whom we have contact.

Pope Francis puts it this way:

> The future of humankind isn't exclusively in the hands of politicians, of great leaders, of big companies. Yes, they do hold an enormous responsibility. But the future is, most of all, in the hands of those people who recognize the other as a "you" and themselves as part of an "us." We all need each other.[103]

The more we reach out to others with love, the more likely others are to "catch" that love and spread it to others. In this way, our evangelization becomes contagious and hastens the day when our country will be truly life-affirming from the moment of conception to the instant of natural death.

Sometimes, the beginning of meaningful change is as simple as extending a helping hand. As Pope Francis attests:

> Good intentions and conventional formulas, so often used to appease our conscience, are not enough. Let us help each other, all together, to remember that the other is not a statistic or a number. The other has a face. The "you" is always a real presence, a person to take care of.[104]

Questions to Ponder

1. How do you define tenderness?

2. What are the ways in which tenderness is part of your everyday life?

3. Ponder the passage from 1 Corinthians 13. In what ways does love manifest itself in your life?

4. How can you extend a helping hand to someone this week?

Chapter 16

And Now a Word from the Holy Father

"The Gospel of life is at the heart of Jesus' message."

— Pope St. John Paul II[105]

When I was working as a reporter, I began to read *Evangelium Vitae (The Gospel of Life)*. The 1995 encyclical was devoted to "the value and inviolability of human life."[106] This trailblazing work by Pope St. John Paul II dramatically altered the way that I viewed issues such as abortion and euthanasia. It was instrumental in transforming me from someone who promoted the culture of death to an individual who embraced the culture of life.

An entire generation has grown up since the writing of this encyclical. Yet, I find that the message of this work is as applicable today as when it was first written. This should not be surprising, since truth is timeless and goodness has no expiration date.

Take, for instance, the issue of abortions performed in response to prenatal diagnoses of chromosomal abnormalities, such as Down syndrome.

The practice continues today, leading to the majority of preborn babies with an extra chromosome being aborted. Pope John Paul broached the subject this way:

> Prenatal diagnosis, which presents no moral objections if carried out in order to identify the medical treatment which may be needed by the child in the womb, all too often becomes an opportunity for proposing and procuring an abortion. This is eugenic abortion, justified in public opinion on the basis of a mentality — mistakenly held to be consistent with the demands of "therapeutic interventions" — which accepts life only under certain conditions and rejects it when it is affected by any limitation, handicap or illness.[107]

The Holy Father extended his concern to those facing the twilight of life:

> Threats which are no less serious hang over the incurably ill and the dying. In a social and cultural context which makes it more difficult to face and accept suffering, the temptation becomes all the greater to resolve the problem of suffering by eliminating it at the root, by hastening death so that it occurs at the moment considered most suitable.[108]

He was prescient when it came to the worldwide movement promoting assisted suicide and euthanasia. Unfortunately, such efforts to hasten death continue, although it should be noted that, in the United States, pro-assisted suicide legislation has been defeated in more jurisdictions than it has been enacted.[109]

Pope John Paul also saw glimmers of hope in the culture which still persist to this day. He viewed the Church as a profound witness to the sanctity of human life:

> [H]ow can we fail to mention all those daily gestures of openness, sacrifice and unselfish care which countless people lovingly make in families, hospitals, orphanages, homes for the elderly and other centers or communities which defend life? Allowing herself to be guided by the example of Jesus the "Good Samaritan" (cf. Lk 10:29-37) and upheld by his strength, the Church has always been in the front line in providing charitable help: so many of her sons and daughters, especially men and women Religious, in traditional and ever new forms, have consecrated and continue to consecrate their lives to God, freely giving of themselves out of love for their neighbor, especially for the weak

and needy. These deeds strengthen the bases of the "civilization of love and life", without which the life of individuals and of society itself loses its most genuinely human quality. Even if they go unnoticed and remain hidden to most people, faith assures us that the Father "who sees in secret" (Mt 6:6) not only will the reward these actions but already here and now makes them produce lasting fruit for the good of all.[110]

Moreover, our faith in Christ can provide us with powerful strength for the challenge of defending human life:

> The unconditional choice for life reaches its full religious and moral meaning when it flows from, is formed by and nourished by faith in Christ. Nothing helps us so much to face positively the conflict between death and life in which we are engaged as faith in the Son of God who became man and dwelt among men so "that they may have life, and have it abundantly" (Jn 10:10). It is a matter of faith in the Risen Lord, who has conquered death; faith in the blood of Christ "that speaks more graciously than the blood of Abel" (Heb 12:24).

With the light and strength of this faith, therefore, in facing the challenges of the present situation, the Church is becoming more aware of the grace and responsibility which come to her from her Lord of proclaiming, celebrating and serving the Gospel of life.[111]

Our efforts to redeem the culture that surrounds us will be enhanced if we adopt a contemplative outlook that enables us to see the inestimable worth of each individual, as the Pontiff elaborated:

Such an outlook arises from faith in the God of life, who has created every individual as a "wonder" (cf. Ps 139:14). It is the outlook of those who see life in its deeper meaning, who grasp its utter gratuitousness, its beauty and its invitation to freedom and responsibility. It is the outlook of those who do not presume to take possession of reality but instead accept it as a gift, discovering in all things the reflection of the Creator and seeing in every person his living image (cf, Gen 1:27; Ps 8:5). This outlook does not give in to discouragement when confronted by those who are sick, suffering, outcast or at death's door. Instead, in all these situations it feels challenged to find meaning, and precisely

in these circumstances it is open to per-
ceiving in the face of every person a call to
encounter, dialogue and solidarity.[112]

With such an outlook, Pope St. John Paul II
noted, we can honor each individual and give praise
for life's precious and priceless gift. We can also share
in the life of grace through Christ our Savior.

Questions to Ponder

1. To what extent is the Gospel of Life part of your everyday existence?

2. How can you act as a "Good Samaritan" for the cause of life this week?

3. How can a stronger relationship with Christ fuel our evangelization efforts?

4. What would it take for you to adopt a "contemplative outlook" in the week ahead?

Conclusion

Go Forth!

"[A]t the origin of every human being there is not something haphazard or chance, but a loving plan of God."

— Pope Benedict XVI[113]

PART 1:
SPIRITUAL ACTION PLAN

Pope Benedict XVI packed a great deal of wisdom in the brief preceding quotation. To begin with, he established the scientific fact that human beings have a distinct beginning — that there is a definite line of demarcation when life begins.

Moreover, the dawn of life is not mere happenstance, but a well-ordered occurrence in the history of humanity. No human being is an accident — we are all the result of careful thought by God.

In addition, our creation is a profound act of love by the Lord — it is His love that led to our very lives and that continues to sustain us.

In order to be effective ambassadors for the cause of life, we must remain ever close to our Creator. We cannot hope to help with the business of saving lives unless our own lives are models of Christian witness.

Consequently, it can be helpful to have at the ready a *spiritual action plan* which will power our works of mercy. This blueprint for holiness will enable us to become, with God's grace, the wounded healers our culture desperately needs.

An effective *spiritual action plan* could include:

A Morning Offering. This brief prayer dedicates our day to the Lord, including our actions and sacrifices as well as prayers of adoration, contrition, thanksgiving, and supplication. Through these prayers, we adore God ... express our sorrow for sin ... thank God for His many blessings ... and ask God for favors, if they be in keeping with His Holy Will.

Daily Rosary. Praying a Rosary each day can yield tremendous blessings upon our apostolic works. If you are in a season of life that does not permit a daily Rosary – such as caring for an infant or for small children – consider praying a five-minute decade, perhaps when you are traveling to complete your next errand. Praying for the Blessed Mother's intercession is a powerful way to fuel our pro-life efforts.

Offering pro-life intentions at Mass. When you attend Sunday or Saturday night Mass, consider praying for pregnant women in challenging circumstances … fathers of unborn children … doctors and nurses … those tempted by the thought of assisted suicide … or other pro-life intentions. If you are able to attend Mass during the week, the Liturgy can further bless your pro-life activities. Because of my current work schedule, I am not able to attend weekday Mass, so I watch it on my computer via livestream on Facebook, DivineMercyPlus.org, or broadcast from EWTN.

Offer your Holy Communion on behalf of an unborn child and the child's family. This is a wonderful way to offer graces for a child who might be in danger of abortion. It may also provide the spiritual courage a woman needs to choose life for her unborn baby.

Engage in frequent Spiritual Communions. Just asking Jesus to come to us spiritually can help us to cope with the trials and tribulations we face each day — especially if we are not in a position to receive the Body and Blood of Christ in Holy Communion at Mass.

Receive the Sacrament of Reconciliation regularly. I try to go to Confession every two to four weeks to cleanse my soul of my sins and to receive the grace to avoid the near occasion of sin in the future. The Sacrament of Penance is a key way to stay close to Jesus as we journey in faith.

Observe a Weekly Holy Hour. If you live near a perpetual Eucharistic Adoration chapel where the Sacred Host is exposed 24 hours a day, consider volunteering for an hour of adoration. In the absence of a perpetual chapel, you may be able to attend an hour of adoration at a nearby parish. If such opportunities are not available where you live, Google "adoration chapel livestream" on your computer. The search results should yield chapels where you can pay "virtual visits" to our Lord in the Blessed Sacrament.

Engage in spiritual reading daily. A number of phone apps can provide you with the readings from daily Mass, as well as words of reflection. You might read directly from your Bible, or from a daily devotional book. The important thing is to feed your mind and soul with treasures that you can contemplate throughout the day. I find my day is simply not complete without 15 minutes of spiritual reading.

Pray and/or study in community on a regular basis. We should not try to travel the spiritual path alone. It is critical for us to connect with other people on our journey of faith. Participating in a Bible study, "Women of Grace" study, "That Man is You" study, or a weekly Rosary group can aid us in our spiritual growth. And with that growth, we are better equipped to minister to people in our pro-life advocacy.

It is also important to connect with trusted online sources such as *CatholicMom. com, National Right to Life News Today, Catholic News Agency,* and *National Catholic Register.* These will provide you with information that will help you to be the most effective advocate you can be.

In order to take your advocacy to the next level, be sure to sign up to receive news and information from your state pro-life group. National Right to Life offers an online list of state affiliates at www.nrlc. org/about/stateaffiliates.

The better informed you are, the more powerful will be your witness to the beauty and sanctity of life!

PART 2:
LIVING OUT THE GOSPEL OF LIFE

When my seventh-grade teacher and school principal, Mrs. Clark, recruited me for the pro-life movement, I had no idea that calling would take me to the corridors of power, from state capitols to the U.S. Capitol Building in Washington, D.C. With my life touched by "The Master's Hand," I have had the opportunity to witness a pro-life bill I had lobbied for signed into law ... see strongly-committed pro-life individuals sworn into office ... and share smiles and an outpouring of joy with people saved from abortion.

Living out the Gospel of Life has brought a sense of peace and purpose to my life that I had hardly dreamed possible. I have found that the cause of promoting life is a noble endeavor which leaves a legacy of love behind.

Now that you have your spiritual action plan in place, it is time for you to discover your own path to living out the Gospel of Life. But how do you find your way? My experience as a pro-life advocate in Pennsylvania has given me insight into how ordinary citizens can achieve life-saving results.

> ***Step One: Self-Evaluation.*** The journey may begin with an evaluation of your skills and talents. Whether your skill set involves writing letters to the editor, crafting fund-

raising appeals, or knitting caps for newborn babies, your contribution is vital to the success of pro-life advocacy. No matter what your particular gift, the pro-life movement can use you!

Step Two: Form a Connection. It is vital that you form a connection with a group such as a state affiliate of National Right to Life. The group can provide you with legislative alerts which will let you know when critical bills are coming up for a vote. The alerts will enable you to contact your state lawmakers so that you can urge them to pursue pro-life policies and to oppose measures which threaten innocent human life.

Step Three: Volunteer! The best way to serve as an Ambassador for Life is to volunteer. Perhaps you can help out with activities such as marches and rallies. With the overturn of *Roe v. Wade,* grassroots action at the state and local level has become all the more important. If you are a specialist in a particular field, such as the law, health care, or even accounting, you can also make a world of difference by volunteering your services to a worthy pro-life organization.

In addition, community-based pregnancy care centers are always looking for people who can donate their time. Whether you engage in counseling or sorting baby clothes, designing newsletters, or distributing diapers, you will be contributing mightily to helping to save precious lives.

Step Four: Educate Yourself. I have to say that, working in the pro-life movement, I learn something new every day. Whether it involves the latest medical breakthrough in saving premature babies or pilot programs to help pregnant women and their families succeed, new information comes my way on a regular basis.

I encourage you to stay up to date by checking out the websites run by National Right to Life's state affiliates. There, you will find a host of information about the latest pro-life developments. It is also important to realize that you cannot hope to educate your family, your friends, and public officials unless you have first educated yourself.

The fall of *Roe v. Wade* has launched a new era in the pro-life movement — one that relies more heavily on community engagement and involvement. With the aid of motivation, enthusiasm, and dedication, we can go forth and bring about the change that will save lives, transform hearts, and revitalize our world. Miracles can and will happen, if only we cooperate with God's loving plan for humanity.

Questions to Ponder

1. Have you thought about your life as being the result of the loving plan of God?

2. What would it take for you to follow a spiritual action plan this week?

3. Are there ways you could re-arrange your schedule to make room for living out the Gospel of Life?

4. Which aspects of the plans listed above can you incorporate into your day during this season of life?

Selected Prayers

A LITANY FOR LIFE

The following prayer, adapted from the U.S. Conference of Catholic Bishops, is based on 1 Corinthians 12:31-13:8a.[114]

Lord, *as You taught us,* love is patient.

Give to the mother who is tempted to abort her child the patience to endure the suffering that will bring forth new life.

Lord, *as You taught us,* love is kind.

Give to the new father whose friends tell him to abort his child the gentleness, compassion and courage to support his wife and child, protect them from all that could harm them, and sustain them against selfishness and hate.

Lord, *as You taught us,* love is not jealous.

Remove from all human hearts the temptation to trade human life for advantage, convenience or personal benefit. Deliver us from the expediency that values personal gain and pleasure over the dignity of human life.

Lord, *as You taught us,* love is not pompous.

Deliver us from the arrogance that sees our needs or wants as superior to the rights of others. Help us to see all our brothers and sisters as worthy of all of our love.

Lord, *as You taught us,* love is not inflated.

Grant us a share in the humility of your Son, who sought not to be served, but to serve. Help us to see in every human life, rich or poor, young or old, guilty or innocent, a reflection of Your image and likeness.

Lord, *as You taught us,* love is not rude.

Implant a spirit of gentle compassion in the hearts of each of Your sons and daughters, Lord, that no person may ever be treated as less than the child of God which You have made them, through the Paschal Death and Resurrection of Your only-begotten Son.

Lord, *as You taught us,* love does not seek its own interests.

Give to all who govern us, Lord, a generous spirit, that our country may not so much seek to be great as to be good, to be rich in possessions as to be rich in mercy, or to be renowned as to be renowned for justice and truth for all.

Lord, *as You taught us,* love is not quick-tempered.

Grant that by our prudence and patience we might learn to live that sacrificial love by which Your Son died for us on the Cross, that all men and women might know our kindness and willingness to love them unto death after the model of our Lord and Savior.

Lord, *as You taught us,* love does not brood over injury.

Give us the grace of mercy, Lord, that like Your Son we might forgive those who sin against us, seeking only their redemption and eternal happiness. Forgive the abortionist who takes the life of an unborn child. Move his heart, grant him the grace of repentance, and give us a full share in Your mercy.

Lord, *as You taught us,* love does not rejoice over wrongdoing.

Help us to seek only the redemption of wrongdoers, Lord, and remove from our hearts all desire for vengeance and hate. Help us to desire not revenge, even for

the horrors of abortion, but the repentance and happiness of all Your children.

Lord, *as You taught us,* love rejoices with the
truth.

Implant deep within our hearts a sense of
the joy of the Gospel of Life, and make
us joy-filled evangelists of Your great gift
of life.

Lord, *as You taught us,* love bears all things.

When we are insulted or reviled for the
sake of the Gospel of Life, give us the
courage and the innocence of the children
of God. Help us, Lord, to suffer for the
sake of Your truth, and never to seek our
own good, even in the good work we do.

Lord, *as You taught us,* love believes all things.

Deliver us from every temptation to
despair, Lord. When we are discouraged,
give us the grace to trust in Your mercy
and to know that Your love is ever victo-
rious, even in the face of darkness, death,
and hate.

Lord, *as You taught us,* love hopes all things.

As we trust in Your infinite love, O Lord,
give us the trust that comes from the

Gospel, and help us to cling to that sure and certain hope that for those who love God all things come to good.

Lord, *as You taught us,* love endures all things.

In the face of death, destruction, and a culture of death, never let us lose sight of the beauty of the face of Your only-begotten Son, Our Lord, who suffered the torments of His Passion and Death for the sake of our [liberation from] sin. Let us trust that through His Passion we will have the strength to do Your will and to carry each cross that comes our way for the glory of God and the love of His little ones.

Lord, *as You taught us,* love never fails.

When the crusade for life seems unending and our latest initiatives have failed, when our hearts are filled with sadness or anger or fear, come to our aid, O Lord, and give us the assurance that You are ever with us, that Your mercies will not end, and that You, our Creator and our God, will bring victory to all who seek to love as You have commanded them.

LITANY TO THE DIVINE MERCY

Taken from St. Maria Faustina Kowalska's diary, *Divine Mercy in My Soul.*[115]

The Response is: **I trust in You.**

Divine Mercy, gushing forth from the bosom of the Father, **I trust in You**.

Divine Mercy, greatest attribute of God, **R.**

Divine Mercy, incomprehensible mystery, **R.**

Divine Mercy, fountain gushing forth from the mystery of the Most Blessed Trinity, **R.**

Divine Mercy, unfathomed by any intellect, human or angelic, **R.**

Divine Mercy, from which wells forth all life and happiness, **R.**

Divine Mercy, better than the heavens, **R.**

Divine Mercy, source of miracles and wonders, **R.**

Divine Mercy, encompassing the whole universe, **R.**

Divine Mercy, descending to earth in the Person of the Incarnate Word, **R.**

Divine Mercy, which flowed out from the open wound of the Heart of Jesus, **R.**

Divine Mercy, enclosed in the Heart of Jesus for us, and especially for sinners, **R.**

Divine Mercy, unfathomed in the institution of
the Sacred Host, **R.**

Divine Mercy, in the founding of the
Holy Church, **R.**

Divine Mercy, in the Sacrament of Holy
Baptism, **R.**

Divine Mercy, in our justification through
Jesus Christ, **R.**

Divine Mercy, accompanying us through our
whole life, **R.**

Divine Mercy, embracing us especially at the
hour of death, **R.**

Divine Mercy, endowing us with immortal
life, **R.**

Divine Mercy, accompanying us every moment
of our life, **R.**

Divine Mercy, shielding us from the fire
of hell, **R.**

Divine Mercy, in the conversion of hardened
sinners, **R.**

Divine Mercy, astonishment for Angels,
incomprehensible to Saints, **R.**

Divine Mercy, unfathomed in all the mysteries
of God, **R.**

Divine Mercy, lifting us out of every misery, **R.**

Divine Mercy, source of our happiness
and joy, **R.**

Divine Mercy, in calling us forth from
nothingness to existence, **R.**

Divine Mercy, embracing all the works of
His hands, **R.**

Divine Mercy, crown of all God's handiwork, **R.**

Divine Mercy, in which we are all immersed, **R.**

Divine Mercy, sweet relief for anguished
hearts, **R.**

Divine Mercy, only hope of despairing souls, **R.**

Divine Mercy, repose of hearts, peace amidst
fear, **R.**

Divine Mercy, delight and ecstasy of holy
souls, **R.**

Divine Mercy, inspiring hope against all
hope, **R.**

Let us pray:

Eternal God, in Whom mercy is endless
and the treasury of compassion inexhaust-
ible, look kindly upon us and increase Your
mercy in us, that in difficult moments we
might not despair nor become despon-
dent, but with great confidence submit
ourselves to Your holy will, which is Love
and Mercy itself. Amen.

A PRAYER FOR PREGNANT MOTHERS[116]

O Blessed Mother, you received the good news of the incarnation of Christ, your Son, with faith and trust. Grant your protection to all pregnant mothers facing difficulties.

Guide us as we strive to make our parish communities places of welcome and assistance for mothers in need. Help us become instruments of God's love and compassion.

Mary, Mother of the Church, graciously help us build a culture of life and a civilization of love, together with all people of good will, to the praise and glory of God, the Creator and lover of life. Amen.

LITANY OF THE BLESSED VIRGIN MARY, MOTHER OF LIFE

The Response is: **Mary, pray for us.**[117]

Mary, Mother of all Life,
> help us to respect human life from the moment of conception to the moment of natural death. **R.**

Mary, Mother of Compassion,
> you showed us how valuable a single life can be;
> help us to guard and protect the lives of all people entrusted to our care. **R.**

Mary, Mother of the Child Jesus,
> with St. Joseph you formed the Holy Family.
> Guard and protect all families in this earthly
> life. **R.**

Mary, Mother Most Holy,
> you sanctified the vocation of motherhood;
> pour out your heavenly aid on all mothers
> and help them to be holy. **R.**

Mary, Mother of Sorrows,
> Simeon's prophecy foretold that a sword of
> suffering would pierce your heart;
> bring comfort and hope to all mothers who
> suffer over their children. **R.**

Mary, Full of Grace,
> you had a choice in responding to God's call;
> help us always to say "Yes" to the will of
> God in our lives,
> and strive always to do whatever he tells us. **R.**

Mary, Comforter of the Afflicted,
> [call] forth [God's] heavenly grace on all
> who are in need of God's healing,
> especially those involved in abortion;
> help them to experience the love and mercy
> of Christ, your Son. **R.**

Mary, Intercessor and Advocate,
> we lift up the poor, the displaced, the mar-
> ginalized and vulnerable members of society;

Help them to never abandon hope,
but to place their trust in the God
who gave them life. **R.**

Mary, Mother of the Word Incarnate,
you bore in your womb Him whom the
heavens cannot contain;
help us to bear witness to Christ by the
example of our lives and show the world
the extravagant love of God. **R.**

All:

Remember, O most gracious Virgin Mary,
that never was it known that anyone who
fled to your protection, implored your
help, or sought your intercession was left
unaided. Inspired with this confidence,
we fly unto you, O Virgin of virgins, our
Mother. To you we come, before you we
stand, sinful and sorrowful. O Mother of
the Word Incarnate, despise not our petitions, but in your mercy hear and answer
them. Amen.

LITANY OF THE IMMACULATE HEART OF MARY

Written by St. John Henry Cardinal Newman.[118]

Lord, have mercy on us.
Christ, have mercy on us.

Lord, have mercy on us.

Christ, hear us. *Christ, graciously hear us.*

God the Father of Heaven, *Have mercy on us.*

God the Son, Redeemer of the world,
Have mercy on us.

God the Holy Ghost, *Have mercy on us.*

Holy Trinity, One God, *Have mercy on us.*

Heart of Mary, *Pray for us.*

Heart of Mary, like unto the Heart of God,
Pray for us.

Heart of Mary, united to the Heart of Jesus,
Pray for us.

Heart of Mary, instrument of the Holy Ghost,
Pray for us.

Heart of Mary, sanctuary of the Divine Trinity,
Pray for us.

Heart of Mary, tabernacle of God Incarnate,
Pray for us.

Heart of Mary, immaculate from thy creation,
Pray for us.

Heart of Mary, full of grace, *Pray for us.*

Heart of Mary, blessed among all hearts,
Pray for us.

Heart of Mary, throne of glory, *Pray for us.*

Heart of Mary, most humble, *Pray for us.*

Heart of Mary, holocaust of Divine Love,
Pray for us.

Heart of Mary, fastened to the Cross with
Jesus Crucified, *Pray for us.*

Heart of Mary, comfort of the afflicted,
Pray for us.

Heart of Mary, refuge of sinners, *Pray for us.*

Heart of Mary, hope of the agonizing,
Pray for us.

Heart of Mary, seat of mercy, *Pray for us.*

Lamb of God, Who takes away the sins of the
world, *Spare us, O Lord.*

Lamb of God, Who takes away the sins of the
world, *Graciously hear us, O Lord.*

Lamb of God, Who takes away the sins of the
world, *Have mercy on us.*

V. Immaculate Mary, meek and humble of heart,

R. *Make our hearts like unto the Heart of Jesus.*

Let us pray:

O most merciful God, Who, for the salvation of sinners and the refuge of the
miserable, was pleased that the Most

Pure Heart of Mary should be most like in charity and pity to the Divine Heart of Thy Son, Jesus Christ, grant that we, who commemorate this sweet and loving Heart, by the merits and intercession of the same Blessed Virgin, may merit to be found like unto the Heart of Jesus, through the same Christ Our Lord.

R. *Amen.*

Additional Resources

HELPFUL BOOKS

Chautard, Jean-Baptist. *The Soul of the Apostolate.* Tan Books: 1946.

Fleming, Maureen C. *Discovering Emmanuel: A Path to a Deeper Relationship with Christ.* Marian Press: 2020.

Gaitley, Fr. Michael E., MIC. *33 Days to Morning Glory.* Marian Press: 2012.

_____. *33 Days to Morning Glory: Group Retreat and Study Guide.* Marian Press: 2023.

Gallagher, Maria V. *Joyful Encounters with Mary: A Woman's Guide to Living the Mysteries of the Rosary.* Marian Press: 2022.

Kowalska, St. Maria Faustina. *The Diary of Saint Mary Faustina Kowalska – Divine Mercy in My Soul.* Marian Press: 2000.

BENEFICIAL WEBSITES

The Holy See – Vatican: www.vatican.va/content/vatican/en.html

Catholic News Agency: www.CatholicNewsAgency.com

Marians of the Immaculate Conception: www.Marian.org

The Divine Mercy: www.TheDivineMercy.org, DivineMercyPlus.org

Eternal Word Television Network: www.ewtn.com

National Catholic Register: www.ncregister.com

ENLIGHTENING PODCASTS

Positively Pro-Life with Maria V. Gallagher:
gallagherm.podbean.com

Available on www.DivineMercyPlus.org/Podcasts:
Explaining the Faith with Fr. Chris Alar, MIC
The Imitation of Christ by Thomas A. Kempis
with Fr. Joe Roesch, MIC
Saint Faustina's Diary in a Year with Fr. Joe
Roesch, MIC
Sparks of Mercy with Chris Sparks

INFORMATIVE VIDEOS

Alar, Fr. Chris, MIC. "40 Hours Devotion —
Eucharistic Miracles and St. Kateri." February 9,
2022. www.youtube.com/watch?v=O4cwXJBRskk

_____. "Explaining the Faith — Why the
Church is Pro-Life: Understanding and
Explaining It." January 15, 2022.
www.DivineMercyPlus.org/videos/why-church-
pro-life-understanding-and-explaining-it

_____ . "Explaining the Faith — Understanding Divine Mercy — Part 1: What Is It?"
April 9, 2022. www.DivineMercyPlus.org/
videos/understanding-divine-mercy-part-1-what-it

Robertson, Prudence. "EWTN Pro-Life Weekly."
June 2, 2022. www.youtube.com/watch?v=
el5wsitPxcw

Tomeo, Teresa. "Life After Roe: How Pro-Life
Leaders in Michigan Fight for the Unborn."
EWTN News in Depth. June 10, 2022.
www.youtube.com/watch?v=BrmrEH1t4eI

Acknowledgments

I offer gracious thanks to the fantastic publishing team at Marian Press that shepherded this book from concept to publication, especially Dr. Joe McAleer, Kaitlin Stasinski, Chris Sparks, and Dr. Robert Stackpole.

Thank you as well to my pro-life colleagues, who inspire me each day.

I am also indebted to the members of my Cursillo prayer team, who have faithfully stood by me in the most difficult times.

Thank you to my sister, Terri, who is a constant source of support.

I offer a heart filled with gratitude to my lovely daughter, Gabriella, who makes the world a better place just by her presence.

I thank the Blessed Mother and St. Joseph for serving as faithful protectors for my family.

Finally, all praise to the Father, the Son, and the Holy Spirit, who shower me with love each day.

About the Author

Maria V. Gallagher serves as an advocate for pregnant women, their babies, people with disabilities, and the frail elderly. Prior to her advocacy work, Maria worked as a radio reporter and television news producer.

Maria is the author of the book *Joyful Encounters with Mary: A Woman's Guide to Living the Mysteries of the Rosary* (Marian Press, 2022). Her writing has also appeared on *CatholicMom.com*, *LifeNews.com*, and on the *National Right to Life News Today* website. Maria is a co-host of the podcast *Positively Pro-Life!* and is the mother of one beautiful ballerina. She makes her home in central Pennsylvania.

Notes

[1] Maria Faustina Kowalska, *Diary of Saint Maria Faustina Kowalska: Divine Mercy in My Soul* (Stockbridge: Marian Press, 1987), 303.

[2] Laura Hensley, "12 Times the Saints Dropped Some Serious Truth Bombs," Epic, https://epicpew.com/saints-truth-bombs/

[3] *Catechism of the Catholic Church*, #2013; www.usccb.org/beliefs-and-teachings/what-we-believe/catechism/catechism-of-the-catholic-church

[4] Ibid., #2626.

[5] Ibid., #2627

[6] Ibid., #2628.

[7] Ibid., #2629.

[8] Ibid., #2631.

[9] Ibid., #2633.

[10] Ibid., #2635.

[11] Ibid., #2636.

[12] Ibid., #2638.

[13] Ibid., #2639.

[14] Ibid., #1324

[15] Ibid.

[16] *CCC*, #1327.

[17] Fr. John A. Hardon, "There is No Stopping Abortion without the Eucharist," The Real Presence Association, www.therealpresence.org/archives/Abortion_Euthanasia/Abortion_Euthanasia_003.htm

[18] *CCC*, #1380.

[19] "Spiritual Communion," Harrisburg Diocese, www.hbgdiocese.org/wp-content/uploads/2020/07/Spiritual-Communion.pdf

[20] "St. Therese and Healing of Broken Hearts," Society of the Little Flower, www.littleflower.org/prayers/healing-prayers/st-therese-and-healing-of-broken-hearts/

[21] Rachel's Vineyard, www.rachelsvineyard.org

22 "Becky's Story," Undefeated Courage, www.undefeatedcourage.org/beckys-story.html

23 *Diary of Saint Maria Faustina Kowalska,* 1507.

24 Ibid., 1074, 699, 1485, 1578.

25 Pope John Paul II, *Veritatis Splendor,* www.Marian.org/articles/mary-mother-mercy-her-unequalled-role-gods-plan

26 "Our Lady of Guadalupe," *Catholic Digest,* www.catholicdigest.com/from-the-magazine/quiet-moment/our-lady-of-guadalupe-i-am-your-merciful-mother

27 *CCC,* #508.

28 Ibid., #969.

29 Ibid., #963.

30 Ibid., #971.

31 "Daily Rosary," St. Mary Woodstock, www.stmary-woodstock.org/prayer/17-daily-rosary

32 Ibid.

33 Ibid.

34 Ibid.

35 "Mother's Day: 12 Catholic Quotes on the Beauty of Motherhood," Catholic News Agency, www.catholicnewsagency.com/news/247583/mothers-day-12-catholic-quotes-on-the-beauty-of-motherhood

36 "Mother Teresa Acceptance Speech," The Nobel Prize Organization, www.nobelprize.org/prizes/peace/1979/teresa/acceptance-speech

37 Ibid.

38 Ibid.

39 Dorothy Day, "The Final Word is Love," Catholic Worker Movement, www.catholicworker.org/dorothyday/articles/867.html

40 Pope Francis, "Address of the Holy Father," The Vatican, www.vatican.va/content/francesco/en/speeches/2015/september/documents/papa-francesco_20150924_usa-us-congress.html

41 "Holiness is Like Salt," CatholicLink, https://catholic-link.org/quotes/holiness-sanctity-fulton-sheen

[42] Patti Maguire Armstrong, "Venerable Fulton Sheen Warns About Infanticide," *National Catholic Register*, www.ncregister.com/blog/venerable-fulton-sheen-warns-about-infanticide

[43] Archbishop Fulton Sheen, "Prayer to Spiritually Adopt an Unborn Child," https://celebratesheen.com/prayers-2

[44] Michael J. New, "Hyde @40," Charlotte Lozier Institute, https://lozierinstitute.org/hyde-40-analyzing-the-impact-of-the-hyde-amendment-with-july-2020-addendum

[45] Bishop Edward M. Rice, "Abortion Has Effect on Human Family," Diocese of Springfield-Cape Girardeau, https://dioscg.org/abortion-has-affect-on-the-human-family

[46] "Saint Louis de Montfort – His Wisdom in 20 Quotations," https://bigccatholics.blogspot.com/2017/04/saint-louis-de-monfort-his-wisdom-in-20.html

[47] "Positively Pro-Life Podcast," Pennsylvania Pro-Life Federation, https://wwdbam.com/shows/positively-pro-life/podcasts

[48] "Prenatal Diagnosis of Down Syndrome," *Prenatal Diagnosis*, https://obgyn.onlinelibrary.wiley.com/doi/full/10.1002/pd.2910

[49] Missionaries of the Poor, https://missionariesofthepoor.org/doing-small-things-with-great-love2

[50] Paul Kengor and Patricia Clark Doerner, "Reagan's Darkest Hour," *National Review*, www.nationalreview.com/2008/01/reagans-darkest-hour-paul-kengor-patricia-clark-doerner

[51] Acts 22:6-10.

[52] Acts 22:12-16.

[53] Lk 8:1-2.

[54] Mk 16:9-10.

[55] Abby Johnson, "Thanks for Stopping By," https://abbyj.com/thanks-for-stopping-by-1

[56] "Witness #1: Dr. Bernard Nathanson," The Life Institute, https://thelifeinstitute.net/learning-centre/abortion-facts/witnesses/dr-bernard-nathanson

[57] *Diary of Saint Maria Faustina Kowalska,* 848.

[58] Mike Hayes, "What is the Prayer of Absolution?" Busted Halo, https://bustedhalo.com/questionbox/what-is-the-prayer-of-absolution

[59] Mt 5:39.

[60] Col 4:5-6.

[61] "Prayer to be Merciful to Others," Congregation of Marian Fathers of the Immaculate Conception, www.TheDivineMercy. org/message/spirituality/prayer

[62] Jn 4:7-14.

[63] Pope St. John Paul II, Shrine of Divine Mercy in Cracow, Poland, June 7, 1997; www.TheDivineMercy.org/message/ john-paul-ii/quotes

[64] "Why Divine Mercy Matters," Congregation of Marian Fathers of the Immaculate Conception, www.TheDivineMercy. org/articles/why-divine-mercy-matters

[65] *Diary of Saint Maria Faustina Kowalska,* 699.

[66] Father Michael Gaitley, MIC, "What is Divine Mercy?" Congregation of Marian Fathers of the Immaculate Conception, Marian.org/divine-mercy/what-is-it

[67] Ibid.

[68] *Diary of Saint Maria Faustina Kowalska,* 811.

[69] "The Divine Mercy Novena of Chaplets," Congregation of Marian Fathers of the Immaculate Conception, www.TheDivineMercy.org/message/devotions/novena

[70] Alyssa Murphy, "17 Inspiring Quotes from Carlo Acutis," *National Catholic Register,* www.ncregister.com/blog/17-inspiring-quotes-from-carlo-acutis

[71] *CCC,* #2272.

[72] Ibid.

[73] "U.S. Abortion Statistics," Abortion73.com, https://abort73. com/abortion_facts/us_abortion_statistics

[74] Tony Lauinger, "U.S. Supreme Court Case Pending; Democracy May Be Restored to Protecting the Unborn Child," NRL News, www.nationalrighttolifenews.org/2022/05/u-s-supreme-court-case-pending-democracy-may-be-restored-to-protecting-the-unborn-child

[75] Dave Andrusko, "NRLC's 7th Annual 'The State of Abortion in America," 2020: Part 1," NRL News Today, www.nationalrighttolifenews.org/2020/01/nrlcs-7th-annual-

the-state-of-abortion-in-america-2020-part-one

76 "The Voyage of Life," Charlotte Lozier Institute, https://lozierinstitute.org/fetal-development/week-7-to-8

77 "Induced Abortion in the United States," Guttmacher Institute, www.guttmacher.org/fact-sheet/induced-abortion-united-states

78 L.E.A.R.N. Northeast, http://blackgenocide.org/home.html

79 Ibid.

80 "What is the Abortion Pill?" Abortion Pill Reversal Network, https://abortionpillreversal.com/the-abortion-pill

81 "How Do I Start the Abortion Pill Reversal Process?" Abortion Pill Reversal Network, https://abortionpillreversal.com/abortion-pill-reversal/overview

82 Moira Gaul, "Fact Sheet: Pregnancy Centers—Serving Women and Saving Lives (2020 Study)," Charlotte Lozier Institute, https://lozierinstitute.org/fact-sheet-pregnancy-centers-serving-women-and-saving-lives-2020/

83 Patients' Rights Action Fund, https://patientsrightsaction.org/dangers

84 "Read Excerpts from *After Suicide: There's Hope for Them and for You*," Congregation of Marian Fathers, www.TheDivineMercy.org/articles/read-excerpts-after-suicide-theres-hope-them-and-you

85 *CCC*, #2276-2277.

86 Ibid., #2278.

87 "Letter of Pope John Paul II to Women," www.vatican.va/content/john-paul-ii/en/letters/1995/documents/hf_jp-ii_let_29061995_women.html

88 Ibid.

89 Ibid.

90 Ibid.

91 John Paul II, "Apostolic Letter Mulieris Dignitatem," www.vatican.va/content/john-paul-ii/en/apost_letters/1988/documents/hf_jp-ii_apl_19880815_mulieris-dignitatem.html

92 Chloe Langr, "8 Inspiring Quotes from St. Maximilian Kolbe, Martyr of Charity," Epic, https://epicpew.com/saintmaximiliankolbequotes

[93] "Men and the Abortion Aftermath," Zenit International News Agency, www.ewtn.com/catholicism/library/men-and-the-abortion-aftermath-4021

[94] Ibid.

[95] Vincent Rue, "The Hollow Men: Male Grief & Trauma Following Abortion," www.usccb.org/committees/pro-life-activities/hollow-men-male-grief-trauma-following-abortion

[96] "Knights: 80 Percent of Women Reconsider Abortion After Ultrasound," *The Catholic Accent*, www.bluetoad.com/publication/?i=291912&article_id=2407450

[97] "Jon's 2022 March for Life Testimony," "Silent No More Awareness," https://silentnomoreawareness.org/testimonies/testimony.aspx?ID=4287

[98] "Scott's 2019 March for Life Ottawa Testimony," Silent No More Awareness, https://silentnomoreawareness.org/testimonies/testimony.aspx?ID=4158

[99] "David's 2019 March for Life Ottawa Testimony," Silent No More Awareness, https://silentnomoreawareness.org/testimonies/testimony.aspx?ID=4154

[100] "10 of Mother Teresa's Most Memorable Quotes," Catholic Online, www.catholic.org/news/hf/family/story.php?id=70653

[101] "Pope Urges Young People to be Part of a 'Revolution of Tenderness'", Vatican News, www.vaticannews.va/en/pope/news/2019-09/pope-young-people-audience-portugal-solidarity.html

[102] Paul Parker, "Tuesday reflection: 'The Revolution of Tenderness Week 10: May 24-30," Society of the Sacred Heart, https://rscj.org/spirituality/revealing-gods-love-in-the-midst-of-uncertainty/tuesday-reflection-the-revolution-of

[103] "Another papal first: Pope Francis gives TED Talk on 'The Future You," Aleteia, https://aleteia.org/2017/04/26/another-papal-first-pope-francis-gives-ted-talk-on-the-future-you

[104] Ibid.

[105] John Paul II, *Evangelium Vitae*, www.vatican.va/content/john-paul-ii/en/encyclicals/documents/hf_jp-ii_enc_25031995_evangelium-vitae.html

[106] Ibid.

[107] Ibid.

[108] Ibid.

[109] "Attempts to Legalize," Patients' Rights Council, www.patientsrightscouncil.org/site/failed-attempts-usa

[110] *Evangelium Vitae*, 27.

[111] Ibid.

[112] Ibid.

[113] "Pope Emeritus Benedict XVI on the Crisis of Fatherhood," Patheos, www.patheos.com/blogs/faithonthecouch/2014/05/pope-emeritus-benedict-xvi-on-the-crisis-of-fatherhood

[114] Adapted from "A Litany for Life," www.usccb.org/prayers/litany-life

[115] Adapted from the *Diary of Saint Maria Faustina Kowalska*, 949-950.

[116] "A Prayer for Pregnant Mothers," www.usccb.org/committees/pro-life-activities/prayer-pregnant-mothers

[117] "Litany of the Blessed Virgin Mary, Mother of Life," www.usccb.org/prayers/litany-blessed-virgin-mary-mother-life

[118] "Litany of the Immaculate Heart of Mary," https://welcomehisheart.com/litany-of-the-immaculate-heart-of-mary

Join the

Association of Marian Helpers,

headquartered at the
National Shrine of The Divine Mercy,
and share in special blessings!

An invitation from
Fr. Joseph, MIC, director

**Marian Helpers is an Association of
Christian faithful of the Congregation
Marian Fathers of the Immaculate
Conception.** By becoming a
member, you share in the
spiritual benefits of the daily
Masses, prayers, and good
works of the Marian priests
and brothers.

This is a special offer of grace given to you by the Church
through the Marian Fathers. Please consider this opportunity
to share in these blessings, along with others whom you
would wish to join into this spiritual communion.

1-800-462-7426 • Marian.org/join

Essential Divine Mercy Resources

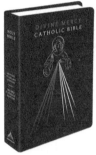

Divine Mercy Catholic Bible

Many Catholics ask what version of the Bible is best to read. In the Revised Standard Version Catholic Edition (RSV-CE) you have the answer.

The *Divine Mercy Catholic Bible* clearly shows the astounding revelation of Divine Mercy amidst the timeless truths of Sacred Scripture. This Bible includes 175 Mercy Moments and 19 articles that explain how God encounters us with mercy through His Word and Sacraments. Leather-bound. 1,712 pages.

Y108-BIDM

Explaining the Faith Series
Understanding Divine Mercy
by Fr. Chris Alar, MIC

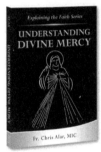

The entire Divine Mercy message and devotion is summarized in one, easy-to-read book! Explaining the teaching of Jesus Christ as given to St. Faustina, *Understanding Divine Mercy* by Fr. Chris Alar, MIC, has it all. Written in his highly conversational and energetic style, this first book in his *Explaining the Faith* series will deepen your love for God and help you understand why Jesus called Divine Mercy "mankind's last hope of salvation." Paperback. 184 pages.

Y108-EFBK

The Divine Mercy

Message and Devotion

The Divine Mercy Message and Devotion

This is the handbook that has introduced millions of souls to the life-changing message that brings hope to a hurting world! Covering every aspect of the authentic Divine Mercy message and devotion — from the Feast and Hour of Great Mercy to the Chaplet and Novena, including selected prayers from the *Diary* of Saint Faustina. By Fr. Seraphim Michalenko, MIC, with Vinny Flynn and Robert A. Stackpole, STD. 88 pages. **Y108-M17**

Call 1-800-462-7426 or visit ShopMercy.org